Marcel Bernad, Daniel Murray

A practical guide to indulgences

Marcel Bernad, Daniel Murray

A practical guide to indulgences

ISBN/EAN: 9783741183065

Manufactured in Europe, USA, Canada, Australia, Japa

Cover: Foto ©Andreas Hilbeck / pixelio.de

Manufactured and distributed by brebook publishing software (www.brebook.com)

Marcel Bernad, Daniel Murray

A practical guide to indulgences

A PRACTICAL

Guide to Indulgences.

Adapted from the Original of
Rev. P. M. BERNAD, O.M.I.

BY

REV. DANIEL MURRAY.

NEW YORK, CINCINNATI, CHICAGO:
BENZIGER BROTHERS,
Printers to the Holy Apostolic See.
1898.

Nihil Obstat.

>C. T. O'CALLAGHAN, D.D.,
>>*Censor Deputatus.*

MOBILE, ALA., August 31, 1897.

Imprimatur.

>✠ MICHAEL AUGUSTINE,
>>*Archbishop of New York.*

NEW YORK, September 10, 1897.

APPROBATION

OF THE SACRED CONGREGATION OF INDULGENCES.

Decretum.

SACRA Congregatio Indulgentiis Sacrisque Reliquiis præposita, cum uni ex suis Consultoribus Opusculum cui titulus "*Guide pour gagner les Indulgences,*" auctore P. Marcel Bernad, ex Congregatione Oblatorum B. M. V. Immaculatæ, examinandum dederit, isque fidem fecerit Indulgentias in eo relatas authenticas reperisse, eadem S. C., præfato attento examine, prædictum Opusculum typis

Decree.

THE Sacred Congregation of Indulgences and Relics, having entrusted the examination of the work entitled "A Practical Guide to Indulgences" (*Guide pour gagner les Indulgences*), by Rev. Marcel Bernad, of the Congregation of Oblates of Mary Immaculate, and having received the report of this examiner declaring he had found all the indulgences mentioned in the aforesaid work authentic, has granted

Approbation.

imprimi ac publicari benigne permisit.

Datum Romæ, ex Secretaria ejusdem S. Congregationis, die 21 Aprilis 1896.

✣ ALEXANDER,
   Archiepiscopus
      Nicopolitan.,
L.✣ S.   *Secretarius.*

permission for the publication of the work on the strength of this report.

Given at the office of the above-named Congregation, at Rome, April 21, 1896.

✣ ALEXANDER,
   Archbishop
      of Nicopolis,
         Secretary.

PREFACE TO THE ENGLISH EDITION.

IT is confidently expected that this work will prove useful to many English-speaking Catholics.

It may be well to state that in the translation the first chapter is entirely new, while the second has been enlarged considerably. The other chapters, however, are practically the same as in the original, and thus the value of the decree of the Sacred Congregation of Indulgences is preserved. One or two slight additions have been made, but these are in accordance with the New Raccolta, which is also recognized as authentic by the Congregation of Indulgences. In translating the prayers throughout this work the text of the New Raccolta has been used wherever possible.

AUTHOR'S PREFACE.

This little work is offered to the public in the hope that it may be found useful by piously disposed persons. There are many indulgences which these persons could gain very readily, but which are lost through lack of a tabulated statement, a spiritual calendar, I may say, in which these indulgences would be set forth in proper order, together with the conditions which must be fulfilled by those who desire to gain them. It is by supplying this want that I expect this book to prove serviceable.

After careful consideration I decided not to insert partial indulgences, except some which are attached to prayers or devotional exercises which many practise frequently. In acting thus I had two main reasons. In the first place, it was my desire to make the work as brief as possible; and in the second place, there are no special conditions to be fulfilled to gain these indulgences. It is sufficient, generally speaking, to be in the state of grace and to form the intention every morning to gain all the indulgences which the Church has attached to the various good works we may perform during the day.

As regards plenary indulgences, I restricted myself to those which are attached to the most commonly practised devotions. It will be a very simple matter for those who are accustomed to other practices of piety, not so generally known, to insert the indulgences attached thereto in the proper place in this little book.

The Church throws wide the doors of its spiritual treasury; and we should not hesitate to use the privileges offered us, both in our own behalf and in behalf of the holy souls in purgatory. Their sufferings are intense, and it is so easy for us to advance the hour of their deliverance!

We should all, therefore, resolve to assist them. Such charity will be certain to meet with a rich reward from Almighty God, and the gratitude of the souls released by our prayers will last forever.*

---

* In compiling this little work I have received much assistance from the book of Rev. P. Beringer, S.J., in its French translation by Rev. Fathers Abt and Feyerstein.

CONTENTS.

CHAPTER I.
	PAGE
INDULGENCES IN GENERAL....	19

CHAPTER II.

CONDITIONS FOR GAINING AN INDULGENCE..	29
Proper Intention............................	30
State of Grace	32
Confession..................................	35
Communion..................................	36
Visit to a Church	37
Prayers	39
Time for Gaining an Indulgence.............	41
Application of Indulgences.................	44

CHAPTER III.

PIOUS ASSOCIATIONS TO WHICH THE CHURCH HAS ATTACHED INDULGENCES	46
Confraternity of the Blessed Sacrament.....	48

Contents.

	PAGE
Association of Perpetual Adoration and Work for Poor Churches..................	48
Association of the Communion of Reparation.............................	49
Archconfraternity of Reparation of Catholic Countries.............................	50
Archconfraternity of the Holy Face........	51
Archconfraternity of the Precious Blood of Jesus Christ...........................	52
Archconfraternity of the Sacred Heart of Jesus (Rome)...........................	52
Archconfraternity of the Sacred Heart of Jesus (Montmartre)......................	53
Archconfraternity of the Guard of Honor of the Sacred Heart of Jesus.............	55
Apostleship of Prayer; League of the Sacred Heart	57
Association of Prayer and Penance in Honor of the Sacred Heart of Jesus (Montmartre, Paris).........................	59
Archconfraternity of Our Lady of the Sacred Heart	60
Confraternity of the Holy Rosary...........	61
Society of the Living Rosary...............	63
Confraternity of the Scapular of Our Lady of Mount Carmel........................	63
Sodalities of the Blessed Virgin	65
Sodality of the Children of Mary Immaculate..................................	66

Contents.

	PAGE
Archconfraternity of the Most Holy and Immaculate Heart of Mary for the Conversion of Sinners	66
Archconfraternities of St. Joseph	67
Society of the Holy Family	67
Archconfraternity of the Holy Family (Liège)	68
Bona Mors Society, or Society for a Happy Death	69
Society for the Propagation of the Faith	69
Religious Orders	70
Third Order of St. Francis of Assisi	70

CHAPTER IV.

SCAPULARS, OBJECTS OF DEVOTION, AND PIOUS PRACTICES	72
Scapulars in General	72
Red Scapular of the Passion	74
Blue Scapular of the Immaculate Conception	75
Scapular of Mount Carmel	76
Scapular of St. Joseph	76
Objects of Piety.—When they Lose their Indulgences	77
Apostolic Indulgences	79
Rosaries or Chaplets in General	81

Contents.

	PAGE
The Rosary of the Blessed Virgin or the Dominican Rosary; The Mysteries of the Rosary....................................	82
Rosaries Blessed by the Crosier Canons......	88
The Way of the Cross......................	88
Crucifixes to which are Attached the Indulgences of the Way of the Cross......	90
The Churches of the Stations in Rome......	92
The Heroic Act of Charity.................	94

CHAPTER V.

THE PRINCIPAL INDULGENCES GRANTED THE FAITHFUL........................	98
I. *Indulgences which may be Gained Every Day*	100
Plenary Indulgences........................	100
Confraternities...........................	100
Scapular	101
Prayers and Pious Exercises.............	102
Partial Indulgences.	103
God and the Blessed Trinity..............	104
Our Lord Jesus Christ....................	105
Jesus in the Blessed Sacrament...........	106
Sacred Heart of Jesus......	109
The Blessed Virgin Mary.................	110
The Holy Family	115

Contents. 15

	PAGE
The Guardian Angel	116
St. Joseph	116
Prayer composed by St. Thomas Aquinas	117
The Souls in Purgatory	118
Various Good Works	118

II. Indulgences which may be Gained Every Week........ 120

Plenary Indulgences........ 120
Partial Indulgences........ 122

III. Plenary Indulgences which may be Gained Every Month........ 123

Those which are Attached to Special Days... 123
Those Attached to Special Days in Any Week of the Month........ 126
Those Attached to Days determined Each Month by Circumstances of Place or Person........ 127
Those that can be Gained Monthly on any Day Selected by the Individual........ 130
Confraternities and Scapulars........ 130
Prayers and Devotions........ 135
Abridged List of Monthly Plenary Indulgences........ 138

Contents.

                                                    PAGE

IV. Plenary Indulgences which may be Gained Every Year.................. 141

Days determined in the Different Months of the Year:

    January 142
    February 146
    March 151
    April 158
    May 161
    June 164
    July 169
    August 176
    September 184
    October 191
    November 196
    December 202

Movable Feasts:

    Feasts and Devotions Preceding Lent 211
    Lent 212
    Passion Week 213
    Holy Week 214
    Easter Season 216
    After the Easter Season 225

Special Occasions during the Year:

    Forty Hours' Devotion 229
    Spiritual Retreat 230
    Local and Personal Feasts 231
    Other Occasions 233

	PAGE
Days Appointed by Superiors	235
Days to be Selected in the Year by the Individual	236
Varying Circumstances of Life	237
Plenary Indulgence at the Moment of Death	238

A PRACTICAL GUIDE TO INDULGENCES.

CHAPTER I.

INDULGENCES IN GENERAL.

An indulgence, in the Catholic sense of the word, is the remission, by legitimate ecclesiastical authority, of the whole or part of the temporal punishment which is still due on account of sin, after the sin itself has been forgiven.

The eternal punishment which mortal sin deserves is undoubtedly remitted when the sin is forgiven, but God requires the repentant sinner to make some satisfaction for the outrage that has been committed against the order of Divine Providence and for the scandal and encouragement in evil habits given to others by sin. Moreover, the temporal punishment by which this satisfaction is made serves to deter the penitent from relapsing into sinful ways, by reminding him that sin always brings suffering in its train.

This suffering may come to us in the shape of physical or mental troubles; it may be satisfied, at least in part, by the patient endurance of the ordinary ills and crosses of this life, as well as by our prayers and good works.

The Holy Bible records many instances of the infliction of this punishment. It will suffice, for the purposes of this work, to adduce those two practical and well-known examples:

In the Book of Deuteronomy, ch. xxxii., vv. 48–52, we read: "And the Lord spoke to Moses the same day, saying: Go up into this mountain Abarim, (that is to say, of passages,) unto mount Nebo, which is in the land of Moab, over against Jericho; and see the land of Chanaan, which I will

Indulgences in General. 21

deliver to the children of Israel to possess, and die thou in the mountain. When thou art gone up into it thou shalt be gathered to thy people, as Aaron thy brother died in mount Hor, and was gathered to his people: because you trespassed against me in the midst of the children of Israel, at the Waters of Contradiction in Cades of the desert of Sin, and you did not sanctify me among the children of Israel. Thou shalt see the land before thee, which I will give to the children of Israel, but thou shalt not enter into it."

Some thirty years, according to the common system of biblical chronology, had passed since the day Moses had doubted, for a moment, the power of God. During these thirty or more years the great patriarch had been much favored by the Almighty, and consequently his sin must have been forgiven; yet here, after this long lapse of time, do we find that God exacts severe satisfaction from His servant for a fault committed in a moment and repented of immediately.

Another noteworthy case occurs in the Second Book of Kings, ch. xii., vv.13, 14. "And David said to Nathan: I have sinned against the Lord. And Nathan said to David: The Lord also hath taken away thy sin: thou shalt not die. Nevertheless, because thou hast given occasion to the enemies of the Lord to blaspheme, for this thing, the child that is born to thee shall surely die." It is equally plain in this instance that David's soul had been cleansed from sin, yet a full measure of temporal suffering was exacted of him to the end that the scandal he had given might be repaired and God's mercy be invoked in behalf of those who had been scandalized.

The Sacred Writings are replete with expressions calling upon sinners to do penance in temporal good works. Hence the prayers, fasts, and the sackcloth and ashes so often mentioned in Holy Writ; hence the various penances voluntarily undergone by the saints of the Old, and especially of the New Law; hence the penances imposed by the priest before he pronounces the words of absolution; hence the days of prayer, fast, and abstinence prescribed by the Church for her children.

The discipline of the Church in these penances was very much more severe in former times than it is now. In the early centuries of her existence many years of penance and trial were required as a public reparation for grievous sin, and the penances were more or less severe in proportion to the guilt of the sinner.

The Church, of course, has never claimed to know the condition of a soul in the eyes of Almighty God, nor the exact amount of punishment which God requires of him who has been forgiven his sins. The public or canonical penances, as they were called, of the early days were prescribed according as human judgment deemed them suitable to the crimes committed, with the knowledge that God would receive them in proportion to their merits, as part, at least, of the punishment due to forgiven sin.

But the Church has not merely the right to exact these penances. It is also divinely empowered to undo these bonds of sorrow and tribulation. "Amen I say to you," said The Master, "whatsoever you shall bind upon earth shall be bound also in heaven: and whatsoever you shall loose upon earth, shall be loosed also in heaven" (Matt. xviii. 18). The Church always reserved the right to release the penitent from all or part of the canonical penance enjoined for sin, on account of the great earnestness and zeal shown by the penitent, or by substituting some other pious exercise for the unfulfilled penance.

Eusebius, in his Church History (book 32), mentions a case in which the whole penance was remitted; St. Cyprian (57th Epistle) tells us that this remission of penance was very common when persecutions broke out against the Christians.* It must be clearly understood that this remission was not merely a release from the performance of the public penance, but,

---
* See also Cyprian, Ep. 15–17 and 23.

through the power given in St. Matthew's Gospel (xviii. 18), the pardon pronounced on earth was ratified in heaven. In other words, God, who is ever faithful to His promises, freed the soul from the punishment from which He would have released it if the penitent had actually fulfilled the penance from which the Church released him. This remission is precisely what we mean by an indulgence, and it is accomplished by the application of the superabundant merits of Christ, His Blessed Mother, and the saints, in behalf of the repentant sinner.

The merits of Jesus Christ, of course, are of infinite value. The Blessed Virgin, although she had no faults of her own to expiate, possessed much merit in the eyes of her heavenly Father for the purity and self-sacrifice that characterized her life. The saints likewise labored in much watchfulness and prayer to attain their salvation, and their merits, at least in many instances, were far in excess of their faults. Now, through the principle of the communion of saints, these inexhaustible merits of Jesus Christ, and the excess of merit won by the Blessed Virgin and the saints, constitute the spiritual treasury of the Church, on which she can draw at will in behalf of her children. The result of an indulgence is thus the same as if those to whom the merit originally belonged directly applied it to the benefit of the person who gains it through the indulgence.

It is needless, therefore, to say that an indulgence is not a pardon of sin. The sin must be forgiven; the eternal punishment due mortal sin must be forgiven before it is possible to gain an indulgence.

Nor is it a permission to commit sin, for such a thing is impossible.* Nor can

---

* When the phrase "remission of sin" occurs in the grant of an indulgence it must always be understood as the completion of the forgiveness by the release of the penitent from all the temporal punishment which follows sin (cf. I. Peter, ii. 24), where we are told that Christ bore our sins in His body on the cross, which cannot mean the actual guilt of sin, but the consequent punishment of the sinners.

an indulgence be bought; the mere fact of desiring or attempting to exchange worldly goods for an indulgence would in itself be a mortal sin, and would thus render the sinner incapable of gaining an indulgence.

Neither can it be said that an indulgence tends to make one slothful and negligent in the spiritual life: on the contrary, it acts as an incentive to virtue. The power to loose and bind is used by the Church, not haphazardly, but in an intelligent manner; and these rewards, held out to us on account of the merits of others, are offered as the guerdons for actions useful and meritorious in themselves. Moreover, these actions must be performed under conditions that necessarily conduce to a more spiritual life. Not every one who performs the prescribed works gains the full indulgence attached. That indulgence is offered for the perfect performance of the work, and God ratifies the Church's sentence by reducing our punishment proportionately to the Church's decree and to the way in which we have fulfilled the action to which the Church attached the indulgence. In seeking this reward, therefore, we have constant reason to increase our piety and fervor.

It may be well also to mention that an indulgence must not be looked on as the value of a prayer or good work. Every good action we perform with the proper intention of honoring God by it has a value in the eyes of Almighty God, and He rewards us for that action by His grace. The indulgence does not affect this reward one way or another, but is an additional reward given by the Church to encourage us still more in the practice of virtuous actions.

If an indulgence remits all the temporal punishment due to forgiven sin it is called a plenary indulgence: a partial indulgence, on the other hand, releases the penitent only from a portion of the punishment which would be inflicted in the ordinary course of Divine Providence.

CHAPTER II.

CONDITIONS FOR GAINING AN INDULGENCE.

In granting indulgences the Church usually prescribes certain conditions which must be complied with by those who desire to benefit by her favors. This is not a case in which good will is sufficient, or in which ignorance is an excuse. The actual benefit of the good work or prayer is, of course, always given by Almighty God, whether an indulgence is attached to it or not, but the indulgence cannot be gained unless the conditions prescribed in the special case are carried out exactly and in the spirit in which the Church intended them to be fulfilled. Sometimes, it is true, dispensations from certain conditions, or circumstances connected with these conditions, are given; but this can

30 Conditions for Gaining an Indulgence.

hardly be called an exception to the general rule, as it is rather a change in the conditions made by the same power which first authorized them.

Some of these conditions are common to all indulgences; so common, indeed, that even when not expressly mentioned in granting a special indulgence, they are understood nevertheless, and must be complied with. These are the two following:

1. It is necessary to intend to gain the indulgence.
2. It is necessary to be in the state of grace.

These conditions must be complied with in every case, whether the indulgence in question is plenary or partial, and no dispensation is ever given from them. The manner of their fulfilment, however, needs some explanation.

Proper Intention.

This intention need not be actually in the mind at the time the indulgenced work is performed, nor need it be put in words as if one was reciting a prayer. It is sufficient that it has been formed at some previous time and not retracted prior to the performance of the action to which the indulgence is attached. The interval, however, should be a reasonable one, and if it exceeds twenty-four hours it would be well to renew the intention. Indeed, it is advisable to form every morning a general intention to gain all the indulgences attached to the prayers and good works of the day: this intention will suffice for the whole day even if the person forming it is unaware of the precise indulgences attached to the day's actions, or if any indulgence is attached to them. This is especially important as regards partial indulgences, as they usually have no special conditions to be fulfilled. Plenary indulgences, except in rare instances, have such special conditions joined to them that the performance of them keeps the intention of gaining the indulgence before the mind.

STATE OF GRACE.

This means that the soul must be entirely free from mortal sin. A person, therefore, who has been so unfortunate as to commit such a sin, and who cannot approach the tribunal of penance before he performs the actions to which the indulgences are attached, must excite himself to perfect sorrow for his sins and resolve to go to confession. Indeed, to gain a plenary indulgence *in all its fulness* it is necessary to feel a hatred for all sins, even venial ones, for as long as even a venial sin remains unforgiven the temporal punishment which it deserves cannot be remitted. A partial indulgence, however, and portion of an indulgence offered as a plenary one, may be gained if the soul is free from all mortal sin, for that is the only sin that deserves eternal punishment, and consequently makes it useless to remit the temporal suffering until the eternal is first done away with by the remission of the sin.

Conditions for Gaining an Indulgence.

A few writers have held that indulgences in favor of the souls in purgatory may be gained by those who are in mortal sin. The opinion, to say the least, is doubtful, and as a general rule the Church expressly mentions either confession of, or at least perfect sorrow outside the confessional for sin, as a condition for gaining an indulgence.

The other conditions which are more or less generally required, especially in the case of plenary indulgences, are usually included under the condition of good works and prayers.

These pious actions must be performed at the time, in the manner, and for the end appointed when the indulgence is granted.

When several of these good works are prescribed they may be performed in the order found most convenient, unless otherwise stated; the indulgence is gained if the person is in the state of grace when the last act required is completed. It must be borne in mind that an action to which

34 *Conditions for Gaining an Indulgence.*

we are obliged in conscience, under pain of grievous sin, does not satisfy the condition for an indulgence; for example, if an indulgence is attached to assisting at Mass, it cannot be gained on Sunday unless two Masses are heard, as one of them is a matter of strict obligation. The communion during Easter time, however, not only fulfils the obligation of yearly communion, but also suffices to gain the indulgences offered on the day it is received. The prayers and exercises of piety prescribed in the rules of religious communities are also sufficient to satisfy the conditions for an indulgence, as they do not usually bind under pain of sin.

If an action is of such a nature that it cannot be repeated on the same day—communion, for instance—or that it would be very unusual to repeat it, as confession, one performance of that action is sufficient to satisfy the conditions required for as many indulgences as are offered for that day, even though all of them, or at least several of them, require it expressly. The other

Conditions for Gaining an Indulgence. 35

conditions, however, must be performed separately as often as they are required for each indulgence.

The good works usually prescribed are:
1. Confession.
2. Communion.
3. Visit to a church.
4. Prayers for special intentions.

At times all of these are required; again only some of them are prescribed; while it happens almost always in the case of partial indulgences, but very rarely for plenary ones, that none of them are exacted.

Confession.

When confession is commanded it is obligatory, even in the case of those who are free from mortal sin. Those, however, who have the pious custom of approaching the tribunal of penance at least once a week (if not legitimately hindered), and who are not conscious of any mortal sin committed since their last confession, can gain all the indulgences offered in the interval without going to confession again. In many places this privilege is extended to those who are accustomed to go to confession at intervals of two weeks. But this is only given to dioceses whose bishops ask for it.

It is always allowed to make the confession the day previous to that on which the indulgence is to be gained.

Communion.

Every confessor has the power to release his penitent from the obligation of receiving holy communion, when it is impossible to fulfil this condition owing to chronic illness or other permanent physical disability. The confessor must substitute some other good work in such a case. Such persons, of course, must go to confession and fulfil the other necessary conditions.

When more than one indulgence (naming confession and communion as conditions) may be gained on the same day or on two consecutive days, the confession and communion of the first day will suffice not merely for the indulgences offered on that day, but also for those of the day following.

VISIT TO A CHURCH.

This visit, of course, must be made in a pious manner, and for the purpose of honoring God, either directly in Himself or indirectly in His saints. If a special church is mentioned, then the visit must be made to that church, and no other will satisfy the conditions for the indulgence unless a dispensation is granted. Members of religious orders are bound by this rule, and a visit to their private chapel is not sufficient for gaining an indulgence unless they are specially exempted by a lawful dispensation.

If a visit is prescribed and no church mentioned, then the visit may be made to any church or public oratory, that is, a chapel which is open to the public and which can be reached directly from a public thoroughfare. Chapels of monasteries, convents, colleges, etc., to which the faithful have not free and public access, are not public oratories, and a visit to them will not suffice except a dispensation is granted. If the visit ought to be made to the parish church, then the person desiring to gain the indulgence should visit his own parish church, or the one of the parish in which he happens to reside for the time being, if he is away from home.

When a confraternity or sodality is canonically erected in a parish or other church, then that church enjoys all the privileges of a church of such sodality or confraternity. When a visit to a church of a confraternity is required, it is expected that each person will visit the church of the local confraternity of which he is a member, but the visit may be made to any church of the same confraternity.

When a person desires to gain several indulgences, for each of which a visit is required, he must repeat the visit for each of these indulgences, nor is it sufficient to remain a long time in the church during one visit. It is necessary to leave the church at the end of each visit and enter again for the next. In case holy communion is received in the church to which the visit has to be made, the prayers may be said at that time and no other visit is necessary, provided communion is received during the time in which the conditions of visiting the church may be fulfilled.

Some other good work may be substituted for that of visiting a church by a confessor, in favor of those who are prevented from fulfilling this condition by chronic illness or other permanent physical impediment.

Prayers.

The prayers required are vocal prayers, but, of course, it is not necessary to recite them aloud. If said aloud, however, they may be said by each person alone, or in company with others; in this case some

40 Conditions for Gaining an Indulgence.

may recite the first half of the prayer and others finish it. It is not necessary to kneel when saying these prayers, unless this posture is prescribed. Neither is it necessary to say them during the visit nor in a church, unless this is specially mentioned.

These prayers are usually prescribed for the intentions of the Sovereign Pontiff; and unless special prayers are ordered, which happens very rarely, it is left to the piety of the individual to select any prayers. It is certain that five Our Fathers and Hail Marys, or any other prayers of about the same length, satisfy the obligation for each indulgence in which these prayers are required.

The intentions of the Sovereign Pontiff are usually the triumph of the Church over its enemies, the uprooting of heresies, the spread of the faith, the conversion of sinners, peace among Christian nations, etc. It is not necessary to remember these intentions, nor to be aware of them; all that is required is to offer the prayers for the intentions of the Pope. Prayers to which one is bound in conscience on other grounds do not satisfy this condition when prescribed for an indulgence.

It is a praiseworthy practice to make an offering every morning of the prayers to be said during the day, to which we are not bound in conscience and which are not offered for other purposes, for these intentions of the Holy Father so far as may be necessary in order to gain the day's indulgences. It will be an easy matter to make this intention at the time of forming the intention of gaining the indulgences attached to the day's works.

Time for Gaining an Indulgence.

Usually a plenary indulgence must be gained on a certain day, and when it is said that the indulgence may be gained during the octave of the feast, the meaning is that it may be gained on any one day during the octave. The strict rule in such cases is that all the conditions for the

42 *Conditions for Gaining an Indulgence.*

indulgence must be fulfilled between midnight and midnight. As has been stated above, it is permitted to go to confession and communion on the preceding day. As to the other conditions, attention must be paid to the terms in which each indulgence is granted.

Sometimes it is allowed to perform the other conditions from the time for first vespers; by this is to be understood the time at which that portion of the divine Office may be recited in public. These vespers may be said any time after noon of the day preceding the feast. During Lent, except on Sundays and the four days preceding the first Sunday, the time is a little earlier.

Again, the time for fulfilling these conditions is sometimes limited so as to begin at sunrise of the day appointed or to end at sunset of the same day. All these, however, are exceptions to the general rule, and are especially mentioned for each indulgence for which they are prescribed.

Members of religious orders gain the indulgence attached to a feast on the day on which the feast is celebrated according to their calendar, but all others can gain the indulgence attached to a feast of a religious community either on the day the feast is celebrated in their own diocese or on the day observed by the community in question. Confraternities and sodalities governed by religious orders enjoy the same privilege.

If a feast is transferred to which an indulgence is attached, and which is observed with solemnity or great pomp (as in the case of a holyday of obligation) the indulgence is attached to the day on which this solemnity is observed even though the Office and Mass of the feast are transferred to some other day. The same rule holds good for novenas, triduums, etc., immediately preceding or following such feasts when indulgences are offered to those who take part in the exercises.

When a feast which is not observed with this exterior solemnity is permanently transferred, the indulgence attached to it is also transferred. If this transfer is not permanent, but merely for the one occasion, then the indulgence remains attached to the original day.

Application of Indulgences.

Indulgences may be gained either for one's self or for the souls in purgatory. It is plain that if a person gains a plenary indulgence fully for himself, or sufficient partial indulgences to remit all the temporal satisfaction which he owes to the Almighty, he cannot gain any further indulgence for himself at that time.

It is well, therefore, to make a special offering, in behalf of the souls in purgatory, of all the indulgences which are not needed for one's self. If a person wishes to offer others for the same intention, he may do so. It is not necessary to make an offering of each indulgence: one act of the will is sufficient to give to one or many of the suffering souls, or to all of them, the benefits of the indulgences that may be gained during a day, week, month, etc., provided such intention be not rescinded afterwards.

It is true that all indulgences are not applicable to the souls in purgatory, but most indulgences can be so applied, and, practically speaking, all those mentioned in this work can be gained for the benefit of the suffering souls.

CHAPTER III.

PIOUS ASSOCIATIONS TO WHICH THE CHURCH HAS ATTACHED INDULGENCES.

A DISTINCTION must be made between the conditions which are required for an indulgence and the actual pious work to which the indulgence is attached. This chapter and the following one, are concerned with these good works.

The Church has been especially generous in offering indulgences to those who league themselves together in pious associations, and the result is that the Catholic world is honeycombed with sodalities and confraternities of various kinds.

There is scarcely any limit to the number of these to which a Catholic may belong; but each one requires certain conditions for membership, and these must be complied with to the letter, unless a dispensation is granted by some one having the power to give it. Moreover, the object of each association must be kept in mind by the members of it, so that their membership may not be merely nominal.

All confraternities, properly so called, have one rule in common, which requires that the names of all members be inscribed on the registers belonging to the confraternity.

The prayers and good works recommended to associates are not necessary in order to gain the indulgences offered members of the association unless the rules expressly state that fact.

In case of lawful impediment, of which the confessor is sole judge, members of these societies may be dispensed from the visit to a church when this is prescribed, but some other good work must be enjoined by the same confessor.

In almost every case a plenary indulgence may be gained by new members of a pious association on the day of their entrance, provided they go to confession, receive holy communion, and say some prayers for the intentions of the Pope.

The following list contains many of the best-known pious associations in the Church, with a brief statement of the object of each, and the conditions which must be complied with by those who wish to be entitled to the indulgences offered in them.

Confraternity of the Blessed Sacrament.

Its end is to honor the Real Presence in the Holy Eucharist, and there is no special condition for membership except to recite once a week the Our Father and Hail Mary five times.

It is necessary that the member should kneel while reciting these prayers.

Association of Perpetual Adoration and of Work for Poor Churches.

The aim of this association is to increase devotion and honor towards Jesus in the

Blessed Sacrament; to repair the outrages that are committed against Him ; and to assist poor churches by giving them gratuitously the requisites for divine worship.

Conditions of Membership.—1. To have one's name enrolled on the register of the association.

2. To spend one hour in adoration before the Blessed Sacrament every month.

3. To make a yearly offering of at least twenty-five cents to assist the work for poor churches. In case of very poor persons, however, the offering may be smaller.

Association of the Communion of Reparation.

Its end is to repair, by frequent communions, the outrages which are committed against our divine Lord, especially in the Holy Eucharist.

Conditions.—1. It is necessary to belong either to the Confraternity of the Sacred Heart or to the Apostleship of Prayer.

2. The full name must be inscribed on the proper register.

3. Each member must promise to receive holy communion on a certain day, either weekly or monthly, for the intentions of the society. In case a member is prevented from making the communion on the proper day, he may fulfil his obligation on some other day of the same week or month, respectively.

Archconfraternity of Reparation of Catholic Countries.

The object of this union is to draw all Catholic nations into one universal act of reparation.

All that is necessary for membership is to visit the Blessed Sacrament on the day appointed for one's country and to pray for about half an hour for the intentions of the union, but the visit may be made on some other day of the week if the proper day is inconvenient.

The days assigned to the different countries are:

Indulgenced Pious Associations. 51

Sunday.—England, Ireland, Poland, and Norway.

Monday.—Austria, Hungary, Germany, and Greece.

Tuesday.—Italy.

Wednesday.—Portugal and North America.

Thursday.—France and South America.

Friday.—Switzerland and all Catholic missions.

Saturday.—Spain, Belgium, Holland, and Syria.

Associates who happen to be in Rome must make the visit on the day set apart for their country in the church in which the devotion of the Forty Hours is being observed.

Archconfraternity of the Holy Face.

The object is to honor a very ancient picture of the holy face of our divine Saviour which is preserved in St. Peter's, Rome, and to make reparation for the outrages offered to the divine majesty.

On the days of the monthly reunions associates can gain an indulgence of seven years and seven quarantines.

Archconfraternity of the Precious Blood of Jesus Christ.

Its object is to honor the precious blood of Jesus Christ, and to offer it to God as a reparation for sin, for the needs of the Church, the conversion of sinners, and in behalf of the suffering souls in purgatory.

Archconfraternity of the Sacred Heart of Jesus (Rome).

The member who desires to gain the two plenary indulgences each month, the plenary indulgence on the feast of the Sacred Heart, and the indulgence for a happy death, must recite daily the Lord's Prayer, Hail Mary, and Apostles' Creed, together with the ejaculation,

"O sweetest Heart of Jesus! I implore
That I may daily love thee more and more."

The most convenient way is to offer with this intention the Our Father, Hail Mary, and Creed at the morning or evening prayers, or at the commencement of the Rosary. The other indulgences offered to the members may be gained without these prayers.

The same indulgences are offered to members of any confraternity of the Sacred Heart, whether it be aggregated to the archconfraternity at Rome, Paray-le-Monial, or Moulins. Those who are inscribed as members of either of the two last may gain one plenary indulgence each month in addition to those offered to the Roman archconfraternity.

Archconfraternity of the Sacred Heart of Jesus (Montmartre).

The objects are: To obtain liberty for the Pope and to safeguard society; to implore the spiritual and temporal favors promised by Our Lord, and which may be needed by associates and their families.

Conditions of Membership.—1. The name of each member must be written in full in the register at Montmartre or in that of a local confraternity aggregated to the one at Montmartre.

2. It contains three grades of membership: Associates, Adorers, and Apostles of the Sacred Heart. Those who are merely Associates undertake to recite certain prayers each day. Adorers are of two classes. Those in the first class, called Daily Adorers, promise to spend one hour during the daytime in prayer before the Blessed Sacrament, or at least before a statue or picture of the Sacred Heart, either every week, month, or three months. Each member can choose his own hour of adoration, but the hour so chosen must be made known.

The second class are called Nightly Adorers, and they promise to pass one or more nights in the year worshipping the Blessed Sacrament, either in the Church of the Sacred Heart at Montmartre or some other church affiliated to it.

Apostles of the Sacred Heart undertake to work zealously to spread devotion to the Sacred Heart of Jesus. The zelators of the archconfraternity naturally belong to this third grade.

All the members of this archconfraternity, no matter to what class they belong, may gain the indulgences of the Roman archconfraternity of the Sacred Heart on the same conditions as they are offered to the members of this last-named association. Nightly Adorers may also gain a plenary indulgence every night during which they spend one hour between 8 P.M. and 6 A.M. in adoration before the Blessed Sacrament exposed on the altar, provided they receive holy communion either on the day preceding or the day following that night.

Archconfraternity of the Guard of Honor of the Sacred Heart of Jesus.

The object of this confraternity is to gather those pious souls who are devoted to the Sacred Heart of Jesus around their divine Master at every hour of the day, to console Him by their loving praise and adoration for the sins and ingratitude by which He is being constantly wounded and offended.

Each member chooses as final, from the twenty-four hours of the day, the one which suits his business and during which he thinks he can more easily be recollected and pious. This hour is marked on a dial opposite his name, and during it he must try to think of our divine Lord, consecrating to Him in a special way all his thoughts, words, actions, difficulties, and love. It is not necessary to spend this hour in church, nor to leave one's occupation. The member is supposed to continue at his daily work, and thus the hour does not interfere with business or other duty.

It is necessary to be lawfully enrolled, and to have the hour chosen written after his name. If it happens that a member forgets the devotion at the proper time, he ought to supply it as soon as he remembers it; but he is not allowed to change the hour without a good reason.

Members of this confraternity have a

right to all the indulgences granted to the Roman archconfraternity of the Sacred Heart, except the one which is granted this organization on the feast of St. Pius V. (May 5th). To gain these indulgences, however, the conditions required from members of the Roman organization must be fulfilled.

The visit to a church of the confraternity which is required for the indulgences may be commuted to a visit to any church when there is no church of the confraternity in the place where the member resides for the time being.

Apostleship of Prayer; League of the Sacred Heart.

The object of this organization is to unite all true Christians with the Sacred Heart of Jesus in praying for the world. To become a member it is necessary:

1. To receive a certificate of admission.
2. To be enrolled on the register of a local centre.
3. To make an offering every morning

of thoughts, words, actions, and sufferings of the day for the intentions of the Sacred Heart of Jesus, the ends of the Apostleship, and especially the intentions recommended by the Pope. A dispensation from the first and second conditions of membership is granted in favor of those who live in missionary countries where it would be impossible or very inconvenient to fulfil them, and also to members of religious communities who have granted the members of the Apostleship a participation in their prayers and good works.

The Apostleship of Prayer contains three degrees. Those who belong to the first degree assume no obligation, save that of making the morning offering as mentioned above.

In the second degree members undertake to recite a decade of the rosary (one Our Father, ten Hail Marys, and one Glory be to the Father, etc.) for the Pope and the intentions of the Apostleship.

In the third degree members undertake

to offer one communion of reparation to our divine Lord, either monthly or weekly, on a day appointed for each member. In case a member cannot fulfil this obligation on the day mentioned, then it may be complied with on some other day of the same week or month, as the case may be.

Associates of the first degree may gain all the indulgences granted to those of the second and third degrees.

Association of Prayer and Penance in Honor of the Sacred Heart of Jesus (Montmartre, Paris).

The object of this association is to repair by prayer and penance, joined to the prayers and sufferings of the Heart of Jesus, all the sins of mankind and the outrages against religion, the rights of the Church, the Holy See, and the person of the Vicar of Jesus Christ.

To become a member it is necessary to be lawfully enrolled, and to choose a special day, either weekly, fortnightly, or monthly, for prayer and penance. On this day the members should offer to God, in union with the Sacred Heart of Jesus and in a spirit of reparation, the whole day, with its prayers, labors, and the difficulties which it may please Providence to send them. They also undertake some mortification of the senses, suitable to their age, health, and condition of life. Those who are engaged in arduous labor are only required to offer the fatigue of the day as their meed of reparation and penance. Associates are divided into three series, first, second, or third, according as they offer a day, weekly, fortnightly, or monthly, respectively.

Archconfraternity of Our Lady of the Sacred Heart.

The object of this association is to honor Mary in her relations with the Sacred Heart of Jesus, and to obtain, through her powerful intercession, a successful termination for difficult and hazardous enterprises.

Any person may become a member of

this association, either by being enrolled by the director of a confraternity affiliated to the archconfraternity, or by sending his name directly to the spiritual director of the archconfraternity, at Issoudun (Indre, France) or at Rome (32, Via della Sapienza). The Holy See allows the associates to visit their respective parish churches instead of a church of the confraternity, on condition that they pay at least one visit a year to the latter church, if there is one of the kind in their place of residence, and the visit may be made without inconvenience. Members of an affiliated confraternity must present themselves in person to have their names enrolled in the books of the local centre, if one exists in their place of residence, in order to enjoy this privilege.

CONFRATERNITY OF THE HOLY ROSARY.

The full name of each member must be entered in the books of the confraternity.

It is not necessary to recite the fifteen

decades of the rosary within the week in order to gain the indulgences of the confraternity.

Those religious who live in the cloister; those who live together in college, seminary, or other religious community, even as domestic servants; members of a Catholic sodality or confraternity, or of any association with a religious end in view, can gain the indulgences which require a visit to a church of the confraternity of the Rosary, by visiting their own chapel.

The plenary indulgence offered to those who take part in the procession on the first Sunday of each month may be gained also by those who are travelling or are in the service of others, and by soldiers if unable to attend; but they must recite the fifteen decades of the rosary in whatever place they happen to be at the time of the procession.

Those who are in bad health or otherwise prevented from attending the procession may gain the indulgence by reciting five decades of the rosary and resolving to go to confession and holy communion at the time appointed by the Church.

Society of the Living Rosary.

This association was first organized by Pauline Jaricot, who also commenced the work of the Propagation of the Faith. The members of the Living Rosary Association are divided into bands of fifteen, and each member recites daily one decade of the rosary and meditates on the special mystery assigned by lot at the first of the month. The indulgences are granted only to those who have recited their decade every day for a month, save where this is impossible.

Confraternity of the Scapular of Our Lady of Mount Carmel.

This scapular, so the tradition runs, was given to Blessed Simon Stock by the Blessed Virgin, who assured him that those who died while wearing it would be saved from hell. Some years afterwards Pope John XXII. saw a vision in which the Mother of God promised to assist the souls of those who had worn the scapular of Mount Carmel during life, and to secure their release from purgatory as quickly as possible, especially on the Saturday following their departure from this world. This great favor is known as the sabbatine privilege or indulgence.

To enjoy the privileges of membership one must receive the scapular from a duly authorized priest and be registered on the books of the confraternity. It is also necessary to wear the scapular constantly, as will be indicated farther on.

The scapular ought to be of a brown color, but black is permissible.

Special conditions are required to be entitled to the sabbatine privilege. It is necessary to preserve the virtue of chastity according to one's state of life, and to recite daily the Little Office of the Blessed Virgin, except in the case of those who are bound to recite the regular office of the Church or the Office of the Blessed Virgin, as either of these offices supplies the place of the Little Office.

Those who are unable to read ought to observe all the fast-days prescribed by the Church, and to abstain from meat every Wednesday and Saturday.

Any of these obligations may be commuted into some other according to the needs of the members, by a priest authorized to do so.

If there is no church of the Carmelite Order in the place where members reside, the visit to the church which is required for many of the indulgences may be made to the parish church.

Sodalities of the Blessed Virgin.

A formal reception and registration is necessary in order to be able to gain the indulgences of these societies. The sodalists can gain these indulgences, no matter where they reside, if they fulfil the necessary good works in the nearest church, or wherever else it may be possible to put them in practice.

Sodality of the Children of Mary Immaculate.

This society is under the charge of the Sisters of Charity. It is entitled to the same indulgences and privileges as the other sodalities of the Blessed Virgin, and need not, therefore, be specially mentioned in recording the indulgences in another chapter.

Archconfraternity of the Most Holy and Immaculate Heart of Mary for the Conversion of Sinners.

It was established by Rev. Father Desgenettes, pastor of the Church of Our Lady of Victories, Paris, and the seat of the archconfraternity is in that church.

The object of the society, as the name shows, is to honor the Immaculate Heart of Mary and to obtain the conversion of sinners through her intercession. Members are requested to say one Hail Mary every day for the ends of the society, but

Indulgenced Pious Associations. 67

it does not seem to be necessary to recite this prayer in order to gain the indulgences.

ARCHCONFRATERNITIES OF ST. JOSEPH.

The best known of these are the ones at Rome (Church of St. Roch), Angers (Church of St. Joseph), and Beauvais (Chapel of the Brothers of St. Joseph).

All that is necessary to be able to gain the indulgences is to have one's name inscribed in the proper register. Members of the archconfraternity of Beauvais are expected to say every day the Hail Mary once, and the ejaculation "St. Joseph, intercede for us" three times.

SOCIETY OF THE HOLY FAMILY.

This society has been re-organized and approved by His Holiness Pope Leo XIII. under the name of "The Catholic Association of Christian Families consecrated to the Holy Family of Nazareth."

Its object is to induce all Christian families to consecrate themselves to the

Holy Family of Nazareth and to take it as their model and pay it due honor. The centre of the organization is at Rome, but every pastor has the power to enroll members of his congregation. The method of consecration approved by Pope Leo XIII. should be followed exactly, and a single family may consecrate itself privately, or a number of families may use the same formula in the parish church in the presence of the pastor or another priest delegated by him.

Archconfraternity of the Holy Family (Liège).

This confraternity is directed by the Redemptorist Fathers, and has its centre in their church at Liège, Belgium.

Its object is to honor the Holy Family, and to encourage the faithful, especially the working classes, to lead a truly Christian life.

It is necessary that the full name of each member be enrolled. If it is impossible to visit a church of the confraternity, the visits necessary for the various indulgences may be made to the parish church.

Bona Mors Society, or Society for a Happy Death.

The object of this association is to prepare the faithful for a Christian death.

There is no condition except that of registration required in order to be able to gain the indulgences.

Society for the Propagation of the Faith.

Every one knows the origin and aim of this pious organization, which has been introduced into every country.

To become a member it is necessary to give one's full name to some local prefect and to say every day one Our Father, one Hail Mary, and the invocation "St. Francis Xavier, pray for us." It is also necessary to give an alms of one cent a week to the society funds, or to give the amount for the whole year at one time. Those who are too poor to give this amount can gain all the indulgences of the society by making a small monthly offering proportioned to their means.

The visit required by the rules ought to be made to a church of the association, or, if there is not one in the locality, to the parish church. Those who live in community may make the visit to their private chapel.

Religious Orders.

As used in this work, the term refers to those religious communities of men or women whose members consecrate themselves to God by the three vows of poverty, chastity, and obedience.

Third Order of St. Francis of Assisi.

Members of the Third Order enjoy all its privileges from the time they receive the habit.

To be entitled to the indulgences they must wear the scapular and cord of St. Francis.

This scapular should be made of gray or brown woollen cloth, and the cord should be of hemp or wool, and it should have from three to five knots. The first scapular and cord are the only ones that need be blessed. Tertiaries are privileged to receive the general absolution, or a blessing with a plenary indulgence attached nine times a year, and it may be given either in public to all the members, or to each individual in the confessional, and in the latter case it may be received on the eve of the feast. Those engaged in daily labors who cannot attend on the feast-day may receive it on the Sunday following or on any day within the octave.

CHAPTER IV.

SCAPULARS, OBJECTS OF DEVOTION, AND PIOUS PRACTICES.

Scapulars in General.

A SCAPULAR, in the original meaning of the word, is a garment which covers the shoulders, and it still forms a regular part of the religious dress in the old orders. In shape it is a long strip of cloth which has an opening for the head, and, resting upon the shoulders falls almost to the ground back and front. The scapular, as it is commonly spoken of to-day, is a modification of this religious garment to suit the convenience of lay persons, and consists of two small pieces of woollen cloth cut in a square or oblong form and connected by two strings. It is worn on the neck in such a way that one piece of cloth falls over the breast and the other on the back.

Every scapular has a special color, suitable to the religious order to which it originally belonged, or to the special devotion it is intended to signify. The pictures which are sometimes seen on scapulars are necessary only in the case of the white scapular of the Blessed Trinity, the red of the Passion and that of St. Joseph. These pictures may be made of any material.

The strings uniting the two pieces of cloth may be of any material and color, except in the case of the red scapular, when they must be of red wool.

Several scapulars may be joined together and suspended from the neck by one string, but they cannot be fastened together at the four corners nor along all the edges; they may, however, be fastened along one side or at two corners. If one of the scapulars so joined is the red one of the Passion, then the string must be of red wool.

The first scapular used is the only one that need be blessed; when that is worn out all the wearer has to do is to procure another and wear it instead of the old one.

The scapular should be worn day and night, and if it is left off for a whole day the person so doing cannot gain any of the indulgences during that day. It may, of course, be laid aside for a short while through any proper motive, such as for the purpose of bathing. Even if a person neglects to wear it for a long time all he need do is to get one and put it on without any blessing or reception.

In the case of any scapular it is required that it be received in the first instance from a duly authorized priest, and that it be worn with piety and devotion.

Red Scapular of the Passion.

The origin of this scapular is said to have been a vision in which Our Lord Himself gave it to a Sister of Charity in 1846, promising at the same time that on the Fridays throughout the year He would increase the faith and charity of those who wore it.

The pieces of cloth and the strings must be of red wool, and one of the pieces must bear a representation of the crucifixion, while the other must have the Sacred Hearts of Jesus and Mary.

There is no special condition for gaining the indulgences. It is not necessary to register one's name.

BLUE SCAPULAR OF THE IMMACULATE CONCEPTION.

It was revealed at Naples in the seventeenth century by Our Lord and His Blessed Mother to the Venerable Ursula Benincasa, foundress of the Theatine Nuns. Its wearers undertake to honor the Immaculate Conception of the Blessed Virgin and to pray for the conversion of sinners. It should be of blue wool, and no inscription of members' names is necessary.

The visit to a church of the Theatines, which is required for many of the indulgences, may be made to any church in which there is an altar of the Blessed

Virgin, in those places where there is no Theatine church.

Scapular of Mount Carmel.

As the wearers of this scapular are organized in a confraternity, it was treated in the preceding chapter.

Scapular of St. Joseph.

The object of this scapular is to honor St. Joseph, the Patron of the Universal Church, and to excite the faithful to imitate his virtues, of which the colors of the scapular serve to remind us.

Form and Color.—The strings of this scapular must be white, and at each end are two pieces of woollen cloth, one of which must be of a yellow, and the other of a violet color. The violet piece is the larger, and the yellow piece is placed in the centre of and sewn on the violet. On one of these yellow pieces is the figure of St. Joseph carrying the Divine Infant on the right arm and bearing a lily in the left hand, while below is the invocation

"St. Joseph, Patron of the Church, pray for us." On the other yellow piece of cloth is the figure of a dove with rays of light, signifying the Holy Trinity, while underneath is the tiara, and below that are crossed keys with a cross between them, and at the foot the words "the Spirit of the Lord is his guide."

There are no special conditions—not even that of inscribing the names of its wearers.*

Objects of Piety.—When They Lose Their Indulgences.

The following are the general rules governing indulgences attached to statues, rosaries, and other objects of piety:

1. In order to receive the blessing and indulgences offered by the Church these objects of devotion must be formed of a substantial material, and not of something easily broken or destroyed, such as paper, pasteboard, cloth, blown glass, plaster, etc.

---

* "Le Scapulaire de S. Joseph," par le R. P. Prosper d'Enghien, capucin.

2. In the case of a crucifix the indulgence is attached to the figure of Christ, and the cross therefore may be of any material, and may even be changed without affecting the indulgence.

3. One article may receive several indulgences, if it fulfils the conditions required for the object to which each indulgence is granted.

4. Each indulgence, however, must be gained by separate prayers or separate good works, as the case may be.

5. Such articles of devotion lose the indulgences attached under the following circumstances:

a. When they are destroyed, either altogether or in great part, or when their nature and form become altogether different from what they had been.

b. When the person who had received them for his own personal use gives them to another, even though the former could use them no longer. If, however, they are purchased, or received, for gratuitous distribution, the indulgences will not cease when such distribution takes place, as in that case the indulgences hold good for the one for whose personal use the objects are first employed.

c. When they are loaned to others with the intention that these others may gain the indulgences attached.

d. They would not lose the indulgences if some one was authorized to purchase them and have them blessed, and afterwards received their actual value; for in this case they do not really change ownership, as the actual purchaser is merely an agent, and acts for another who is, properly speaking, the owner of these articles from the moment his agent buys them.

Apostolic Indulgences.

1. These indulgences are attached to articles of devotion, crosses, medals, rosaries, statues, etc., by the Sovereign Pontiff himself or by some priest to whom he has given the privilege.

2. Those articles of piety which have

touched the holy places and the sacred relics of the Holy Land have acquired, by that fact, practically the same indulgences.

3. To gain these indulgences, besides the ordinary conditions of confession, communion, and prayers for the Holy Father's intentions, it is necessary to carry these indulgenced articles on one's person, or to keep them at home, and moreover to recite, at least once a week, either the ordinary Divine Office; or that of the Blessed Virgin Mary; or that of the Dead; or the Seven Penitential Psalms; or the Gradual Psalms; or the Chaplet of Our Lord; or that of the Blessed Virgin; or the third part of the Rosary; or to be in the habit of teaching Christian doctrine; or of visiting the sick in hospitals, or prisoners, or helping the poor of Christ; of assisting at the Most Holy Sacrifice of the Mass, or of celebrating it, if they be priests.

4. Those who keep objects thus indulgenced in their homes, instead of carrying them about with them, should recite the

proper prayers before them with piety and recollection.

Rosaries or Chaplets in General.

These, as has been already stated in the general rule, should be of a durable material. It is permitted, however, to make them of wood, tin, lead, or even of solid glass. A single rosary may receive the indulgences of St. Brigid, St. Dominic, the Crosier Fathers, the Apostolic indulgences, etc.; but only one of these indulgences may be gained by one recital of the rosary, and that will be the one which the person reciting it intends to gain.

The indulgences and blessing are attached to the beads, and, consequently, the chain may be changed altogether and the indulgences will still remain. Moreover, if one or two beads are broken or lost, new ones may be added, and even though in course of time all the original beads happen to be lost and replaced by new ones, the rosary still retains the full indulgences originally attached to it.

The Rosary of the Blessed Virgin.

1. It may be formed of five, ten, or fifteen decades, and requires a special blessing.

2. The Apostles' Creed, Our Father, and three Hail Marys at the beginning are only an introduction, and are not a portion of the rosary, nor is it necessary to say them.

3. At least a third of the rosary, or five decades, should be said without any notable interruption. Most writers teach that the indulgences are not lost if the interruption is for the purpose of going to confession or communion, or even to hear Mass or perform some other pious work of about the same duration. If the interruption was to attend to some secular business, however, and lasted a considerable length of time, the indulgences would not be gained.

4. Members of the confraternity of the Rosary are expected to recite the full rosary of fifteen decades every week; and

in doing so they are privileged to finish it at their convenience, and they gain the indulgences, no matter how frequently they may be interrupted. This privilege, however, is only for one recital; and if they say the rosary more than once during the week, they should follow the ordinary rule in all cases except the one they say as members of the Rosary Association.

5. In addition to repeating the vocal prayers, it is necessary to meditate on the mysteries of the birth, passion, death, resurrection, etc., of Our Lord Jesus Christ in order to gain the indulgences attached to the rosary. These mysteries are arranged as follows:

Joyful Mysteries.

I. *The Annunciation.* — The Angel Gabriel announces to the Blessed Virgin that she is to be the Mother of God.

II. *The Visitation.*—The Blessed Virgin, on learning that her aged cousin St. Elizabeth is about to become a mother, makes a long journey to visit her.

III. *The Nativity.*—Our Blessed Lord is born in the cave near Bethlehem.

IV. *The Presentation in the Temple.*—In obedience to the religious law of the Jews, Mary and Joseph bring the Child Jesus to the Temple and offer Him to the Eternal Father.

V. *The Finding in the Temple.*—After a separation of three days, Mary and Joseph find Jesus teaching the doctors in the Temple, and explaining the Old Law to them.

Sorrowful Mysteries.

I. *The Agony in the Garden.*—Jesus suffers intense mental anguish, while praying in the Garden of Olives, at the thought of men's sins and the sufferings He will have to undergo.

II. *The Scourging at the Pillar.*—Stripped of His garments, and fastened to a pillar, Jesus is cruelly scourged until His flesh is bruised and torn, and His blood flows in streams from His wounded body.

III. *The Crowning with Thorns.*—The persecutors of Jesus plait a number of branches of long sharp thorns into the shape of a crown, and press it brutally on His head until the thorns pierce His flesh.

IV. *The Carrying of the Cross.*—In spite of all the suffering Jesus has endured, the soldiers command Jesus to carry to Calvary the rude, heavy cross on which they intend to crucify Him.

V. *The Crucifixion.*—On His arrival at the summit of Mount Calvary Jesus is fastened to the cross by long nails, which the executioners drive through His hands and feet, and after three hours of intense agony He expires.

Glorious Mysteries.

I. *The Resurrection.*—On Easter Sunday Christ raises Himself from the dead by His divine power.

II. *The Ascension.* — After spending forty days with His disciples Christ ascends into heaven, accompanied by the souls of the just who had died since the world's creation.

III. *The Descent of the Holy Ghost on the Apostles.*—Ever mindful of the needs of His followers on earth, Christ sends the Holy Ghost to confirm the faith and charity of the apostles, and to preserve the Church in its original purity of morals and doctrine to the end of time.

IV. *The Assumption of the Blessed Virgin into Heaven.*—Twelve years after the Ascension of Our Lord, Mary dies and is taken up, body and soul, into heaven by the power of her divine Son.

V. *The Coronation of the Blessed Virgin.*—Mary is honored by her Son, and is placed in the highest place in heaven after the Blessed Trinity, so that she is Queen over the angels and saints.

6. Those who are incapable of meditating on these mysteries need only recite the prayers; but such persons should accustom themselves, as far as possible, to meditate on the mysteries of our redemption.

7. Any series of mysteries may be taken each day, and the same series may be repeated over and over; still it is more in accordance with the spirit of the rosary to take the mysteries in regular succession, and the following order is generally observed:

Joyful Mysteries—Monday and Thursday.

Sorrowful Mysteries—Tuesday and Friday.

Glorious Mysteries—Sunday, Wednesday, and Saturday.

8. The rosary ought to be held in the hand, and each bead should be touched in regular succession in order to be able to gain the indulgence of one hundred days attached to each Our Father or Hail Mary, and the plenary indulgence granted for one day in each year.

9. When the rosary is said in common by several persons, it is sufficient that one holds the rosary and that the others put aside everything that would distract them, and join in the prayers with attention and respect.

This privilege is only for the ordinary rosary of the Blessed Virgin as blessed and indulgenced with the Dominican indulgences by some priest of the Order of Friar Preachers, or some other properly authorized priest. It does not extend to other chaplets nor to the other indulgences attached to the ordinary chaplet of the Blessed Virgin.

Rosaries Blessed by the Crosier Canons.

These rosaries are indulgenced so that it is not necessary to say the whole rosary, or even a whole decade, as the indulgence is attached to each bead. The beads, however, must be joined together in the usual way, and the rosary must be held in the hand. It is not necessary to make any meditation to gain these indulgences.

The Way of the Cross.

1. When this excellent devotion is performed privately it is necessary to go from

one station to the other until each of the fourteen has been visited.

2. When the devotion is performed by a large number of persons at once, the stations should be visited in like manner so far as the number of persons and the space allotted to the stations admit. When it is impossible for all to go from one station to the other, it is sufficient for the one who is to lead in the prayers, and two acolytes, to go from station to station, and the others should join in the prayers, and so far as possible make some movement of their body by turning towards the station on which they have to meditate.

3. The fourteen stations should be visited without any notable interruption, especially if it be connected with worldly affairs. The Holy See has declared that the indulgences are not lost when the interruption is for the purpose of hearing Mass, going to confession or communion, etc.

4. To gain the indulgences it is necessary to make at least a brief meditation

on the scene of the Passion represented by each station. This is the general opinion, but many believe that it is sufficient to consider one scene of the Passion during the whole time, or even to meditate on Our Lord's Passion in general.

5. There is no prayer prescribed, either before or after this devotion or during the visits.

6. It is very doubtful if the indulgences of this devotion can be gained more than once a day.

7. In the stations it is to the crosses (which must be of wood) that the indulgences are attached. The pictures are not necessary.

CRUCIFIXES TO WHICH ARE ATTACHED THE INDULGENCES OF THE WAY OF THE CROSS.

All who are sick, all who are in prison, or at sea, or *in partibus infidelium*, or are prevented in any other way from visiting the stations of the Way of the Cross where they are erected, may gain these indulgences by saying, with at least contrite heart and devotion, the Our Father, the Hail Mary, and the Glory be to the Father, each fourteen times, the number of the stations, and, at the end of these, the Our Father, the Hail Mary, and the Glory be to the Father, each five times, in honor of the five Wounds of Our Lord, and, again, one Our Father, one Hail Mary, and one Glory be to the Father, for the Sovereign Pontiff, holding in their hands the while a crucifix of brass, or of any other solid substance, which has been blessed by the Father-General of the Order of the Friars Minor Observants, or by any priest to whom the faculty has been given. If the twenty Our Fathers, Hail Marys and Glory, etc., be said by several together, though but one hold the crucifix, and the others, not engaged in any other work, recollect themselves for the prayers, all gain the indulgences of the Way of the Cross.

It is to be observed that these crucifixes,

thus indulgenced, after they have been blessed, cannot be sold, or given away, or lent to any one for the purpose of enabling them to gain the indulgences of the Way of the Cross.

Those who are too ill to say these prayers may gain the same indulgences if, having a crucifix, properly blessed, they make an act of contrition or recite the prayer, "We beseech Thee, therefore, help Thy servants whom Thou hast redeemed with Thy precious blood." But if the crucifix used has been blessed since September, 1890, the sick person must make an act of contrition, say the prayer given above, and also the Our Father, Hail Mary, and Glory be to the Father, each three times, or at least follow these prayers mentally while another repeats them aloud.

The Churches of the Stations in Rome.

1. There are certain churches of the Eternal City to which the Pope, clergy, and

people were accustomed to go in procession on certain days. This custom dates back to the early days of the Church. Pope Gregory the Great granted many indulgences to those who visited these churches on the days appointed and prayed there for the intentions of the Sovereign Pontiff. These indulgences were increased and confirmed by many of Gregory's successors.

2. Members of several confraternities have the privilege of visiting their confraternity chapel or church instead of the special church of the stations for the day. The following associations enjoy this favor:

Archconfraternity of Perpetual Adoration.

Archconfraternity of the Sacred Heart (Rome).

Archconfraternity of the Scapular of Our Lady of Mount Carmel.

Archconfraternity of the Holy Family (Liège).

Archconfraternity of a Happy Death (Bona Mors).

All Sodalities of the Blessed Virgin.
Religious Orders.
Wearers of the Scapular of St. Joseph.

3. To gain the partial indulgences all that is necessary is to visit a church enjoying this privilege on the day appointed, and to pray for the ordinary intentions of the Holy Father during the visit.

4. The days appointed for gaining these indulgences are all the days of Lent, Ember Days, Rogation Days, days during the octaves of Easter and Pentecost, the Sundays of Advent, etc.

THE HEROIC ACT OF CHARITY.

1. It consists in a voluntary offering made in behalf of the souls in purgatory to the Divine Majesty, by any one of the faithful, of all works of satisfaction done by him in this life, as well as of all the suffrages which shall be offered for him after death. This offering does not prevent the maker of it from praying for himself, his friends, or any other like in-

tention, as by it he only foregoes that special fruit of his good works which would belong to himself as a satisfaction for the temporal punishment deserved by him on account of his sins.

2. The person making this offering is free to choose the souls whom he desires to benefit by it, or to place all these merits in the hands of the Blessed Virgin, that she may distribute them among the holy souls as she sees fit.

3. A priest making this offering is, of course, free to offer up the holy sacrifice for the intentions of those who ask him to do so.

4. The heroic act of charity is not a vow, nor does it bind under pain of sin.

5. All the indulgences gained by those who have made this offering are applicable to the souls in purgatory.

N. B.—It is sometimes objected that this act of charity does an injustice to ourselves, because it takes away what is necessary to satisfy God's justice for our sins, and so leaves us much more suffering to endure in purgatory than would otherwise fall to our share.

The answer to this is, that even if this lengthening of our own punishment was an assured fact, it would be a small price to pay for the immense reward that God would bestow in heaven on those who performed such an heroic act of charity. But it is not true that those who make this offering will suffer more on account of it, for we may be sure that God would not have it so. On the contrary, He will reward those who are so generous by enkindling such a great love for Himself in their hearts that it will result in a full forgiveness not only of sin, but also of its temporal punishment; and, moreover, He has still the right to make their souls, if they go to purgatory, the beneficiaries of those prayers and good works which the living are continually offering Him.

Besides, those souls who may be released from their sufferings by these heroic offerings will not prove ungrateful, but rather will they constantly intercede for those to whom they owe their deliverance, and will not cease their prayers until the latter are either brought straight to heaven, or released from purgatory.

CHAPTER V.

THE PRINCIPAL INDULGENCES GRANTED THE FAITHFUL.

The lists of indulgences mentioned in the various sections of this chapter are not intended to be exhaustive, for it would be impossible to make them so, even in a much larger volume than this. It is the hope of the author, however, that these lists contain all the plenary indulgences attached to the devotions and associations which are most widely spread in the Church. It would be well for those who use this book to mark the indulgences which they are privileged to gain and which they desire to gain regularly, and it will also be easy for them to make a note, in the proper place, of those indulgences which they are enabled to gain through some other devotions not mentioned here.

There are a great many people who are unable to fulfil the conditions of visiting a church or going to communion. Those who are prevented by any legitimate reason, and who belong to any pious association, as well as all those who are prevented by continued illness or permanent physical disability from complying with these conditions, should remember that their confessors have power to substitute some other good works.*

In the following lists the day on which the indulgence may be gained is given first, then the association or pious work which gives the right to the indulgence, and, finally, the conditions required for gaining the indulgences.

N. B. — " Prayers " or the " usual prayers " mean prayers for the intentions of the Holy Father.

---

* Many confraternities enjoy special privileges as regards these conditions. These privileges have been mentioned under the title of the proper association in Chapter III.

I. Indulgences which may be gained Every Day.

Plenary Indulgences.

1. *Archconfraternity of Reparation of Catholic Countries.*—Conditions: Confession, communion, to pray for half an hour in any church in which the Blessed Sacrament is kept, and, moreover, to make the regular weekly visit of the confraternity to the Blessed Sacrament.

2. *Archconfraternity of the Precious Blood of Jesus Christ.*—Conditions: Confession, communion, prayers, also to spend one hour in prayer in honor of our divine Lord and the sorrows of His Blessed Mother. This may be either mental or vocal prayer.

3. *Archconfraternity of the Sacred Heart of Jesus (Montmartre, Paris).* Nightly Adorers.—Conditions: To spend one hour in adoration before the Blessed Sacrament exposed on the altar between 8 P.M. of one day and 6 A.M. of the next,

and to go to communion on one of these days.

4. *Blue Scapular of the Immaculate Conception.*—Wearers of this scapular can gain every day the indulgences, *a.* Of a visit to the seven basilicas of Rome; *b.* Of the Portiuncula; *c.* Of a pilgrimage to Jerusalem; *d.* Of a pilgrimage to the tomb of St. James in Compostella. Conditions: To say the Our Father, Hail Mary, and Glory be to the Father each six times in honor of the Blessed Trinity, of Mary Immaculate, and for other special intentions.

N. B.—The partial indulgences attached to these visits and pilgrimages may be gained by wearers of the blue scapular as often as they repeat the above prayers, but it is doubtful, to say the least, if the plenary indulgences may be gained more than once in each case. Confession and communion are not required in order to gain these indulgences, but of course it is necessary to be in the state of grace.

5. *Prayer to Jesus Crucified.*—" Look

down upon me, good and gentle Jesus, while before Thy face I humbly kneel, and with burning soul pray and beseech Thee to fix deep in my heart lively sentiments of faith, hope, and charity, true contrition for my sins, and a firm purpose of amendment; the while I contemplate with great love and tender pity Thy five wounds, pondering over them within me, whilst I call to mind what the Prophet David put in Thy mouth concerning Thee, O good Jesus: 'They have dug my hands and my feet; they have numbered all my bones'" (Ps. xxi. 17, 18). Conditions: To say this prayer with devotion before an image or picture of our crucified Redeemer; and, being truly penitent, after confession and communion, spend some time in prayer for the intention of His Holiness.

6. *The Way of the Cross.*—All the faithful who practise this devotion can gain the same indulgences by doing so, that they would gain by visiting the holy places of Jerusalem. These include sev-

Indulgences to be Gained Every Day. 103

eral plenary indulgences, but they can be gained only once a day.

7. *The Heroic Act of Charity for the Suffering Souls.*—All who have made this offering can gain a plenary indulgence every day. Conditions: Communion, visit to a church, and to pray during the visit for the usual intentions.

Priests who have made this act of charity enjoy the personal indult of a privileged altar every time they say Mass for the dead, but this Mass must be celebrated in black vestments whenever the rubrics permit.

8. A plenary indulgence is offered to all the faithful *who feed three poor persons in honor of Jesus, Mary, and Joseph.* Conditions: Confession, communion, and the usual prayers.

Partial Indulgences.

Unless otherwise specified, these indulgences may be gained as often as the prayers are said or the good works accomplished to which they are attached.

I. GOD AND THE BLESSED TRINITY.

1. *The Sign of the Cross.*—Fifty days each time and one hundred days if it is made with holy water. In each case the words must be pronounced, though they need not be said aloud.

2. To all the faithful who shall say, morning, noon, and night, the *Glory be to the Father* three times, in thanksgiving to the Holy Trinity for the privileges granted to the most holy Virgin, especially in her glorious assumption into heaven, an indulgence of one hundred days every time that this prayer is said, at the three aforesaid times of the day.

3. *Ejaculation.*—" My God and my all." —Fifty days.

4. *Acts of Faith, Hope, and Charity.*— Seven years and seven quarantines. Any form of words may be used, provided it expresses the particular motive of each of these three virtues.

5. *Ejaculation.*—" May the most just, most high, and most amiable will of God

be done in all things, be praised and magnified forever."—One hundred days.

II. OUR LORD JESUS CHRIST.

1. For devoutly invoking the holy name of Jesus.—Twenty-five days.

2. "Praise be to Jesus Christ (Forever, or Amen)." If this is said by way of salutation when people meet one another, fifty days' indulgence.

3. "My Jesus, mercy!"—One hundred days.

4. "Saviour of the world, have pity on us!"—One hundred days once a day.

5. "Jesus, my God, I love Thee above all things."—Fifty days.

6. "My sweetest Jesus, be not my Judge, but my Saviour."—Fifty days.

7. "Jesus, Son of David, have mercy on me!"—One hundred days once a day.

8. Litany of the holy name of Jesus.—Three hundred days once a day.

9. "O Jesus, living in Mary! come and live in Thy servants, in the spirit of Thy

holiness, in the fulness of Thy might, in the truth of Thy virtues, in the perfection of Thy ways, in the communion of Thy mysteries; subdue every hostile power, in Thy spirit, for the glory of the Father. Amen."—Three hundred days once a day.

III. JESUS IN THE BLESSED SACRAMENT.

1. *For Assisting at Mass.*

a. The indulgence attached to any good work.

b. Members of any sodalities of the Blessed Virgin gain an indulgence of seven years and seven quarantines if they assist at Mass on week-days.

c. Associates of the Apostleship of Prayer gain one hundred days on week-days and five years and five quarantines on Sundays and holydays.

2. *For Receiving Holy Communion.*

a. Wearers of the blue scapular.—Seven years and seven quarantines.

b. Those who receive communion frequently.—Five years when they go to confession or holy communion and pray for the intentions of the Pope on any day dedicated to Our Lord or one of His saints.

c. Ten years for those who are accustomed to communicate at least once a month and on the feasts of Our Lord, the Blessed Virgin, the Apostles, and the nativity of St. John Baptist (June 24th).

3. *For Visiting the Blessed Sacrament.*

a. Members of the archconfraternity of Reparation of Catholic Countries.—Ten years and ten quarantines.

b. Confraternity of the Blessed Sacrament.—Seven years and seven quarantines; but the visit must be made in the afternoon, and prayers for the usual intentions are required.

c. Archconfraternity of the Precious Blood of Jesus Christ.—Seven years and seven quarantines.

d. For all the faithful who say, six times,

the Our Father, Hail Mary, and Glory be to the Father.—Three hundred days.

e. During the devotion of the Forty Hours' Prayer.—Ten years and ten quarantines for every visit made with true contrition and a firm purpose of going to confession.

4. *Prayers.*

a. " O Sacrament most holy! O Sacrament divine!
All praise and all thanksgiving be every moment thine!"

One hundred days once a day, and three times a day on every Thursday in the year and during the octave of Corpus Christi.

b. " Soul of Christ, sanctify me:
Body of Christ, save me:
Blood of Christ, inebriate me:
Water from the side of Christ, wash me.
Passion of Christ, strengthen me:
O good Jesus, hear me:
Within Thy wounds hide me:

Permit me not to be separated from
    Thee.
From the malignant enemy defend
    me:
In the hour of my death call me,
And bid me come to Thee,
That, with Thy saints, I may praise
    Thee
For ever and ever.   Amen."

Indulgence of three hundred days; after holy communion, seven years.

IV. SACRED HEART OF JESUS.

1. Visit to an image of the Sacred Heart exposed in a church or on any altar for public veneration (the figure of the heart must be visible).—Seven years and seven quarantines.

2. Archconfraternity of the Hour of Guard in honor of the Sacred Heart of Jesus.—Seven years and seven quarantines.

3. *Prayers.*

a. "My loving Jesus! I (N.N.) give Thee my heart, and I consecrate myself wholly to Thee, out of the grateful love I bear

Thee, and as a reparation for all my unfaithfulness; and with Thy aid I purpose never to sin again."—One hundred days, once a day, if this prayer is said before an image of the Sacred Heart of Jesus.

   b. " O sweetest Heart of Jesus! I implore That I may daily love thee more and more."—Three hundred days.

   c. " May the Sacred Heart of Jesus be loved everywhere."—One hundred days once a day.

   d. "Jesus, meek and humble of heart, make my heart like unto Thine."—Three hundred days once a day.

   e. " Heart of Jesus, burning with love for us, inflame our hearts with love for Thee."—One hundred days once a day.

V. THE BLESSED VIRGIN MARY.

   1. *Rosary.*—*a.* For all the faithful.—One hundred days for each Our Father and each Hail Mary. The five decades must be said without any long interruption, and it is necessary to meditate on the mysteries and to have the rosary in

one's hand. An indulgence of ten years and ten quarantines is offered once a day to those who say it in common with others.

b. Confraternity of the Rosary.—One hundred years and one hundred quarantines if they carry the rosary with them. Five years and five quarantines for each bead on which they say an Our Father or a Hail Mary. Fifty years once a day if they say the rosary in a church of the confraternity, in a chapel of the rosary, or any part of the church from which the altar of that chapel may be seen, or, in places where there is no church of the confraternity, in any church.

c. Rosary blessed by the Crosier Canons.— Five hundred days for each bead on which they say an Our Father or a Hail Mary. Five years and five quarantines for reciting the rosary on Sundays and holydays; seven years and seven quarantines for saying it on the feasts of Our Lord and the Blessed Virgin.

2. *The Angelus,* or, during Easter-time, the Regina Cœli.—One hundred days

morning, noon, and night if at the sound of the bell, where that is possible, these prayers are said in a kneeling posture, except on Saturday evening, all day Sunday, and during Easter-time, when they should be said standing. Those who cannot read nor recite from memory these prayers can gain the same indulgences by saying five Hail Marys at the proper time.

3. *Prayers* which the priest and people say after Low Mass.—Three hundred days each time.

4. *Litany* of the Blessed Virgin (the Litany of Loretto).—Three hundred days.

5. *Prayers.*—*a.* In the morning: "Hail, holy queen, mother of mercy, our life, our sweetness, and our hope; to thee do we cry, poor banished sons of Eve; to thee do we send up our sighs, mourning and weeping in this valley of tears. Turn then, most gracious advocate, thine eyes of mercy toward us, and after this, our exile, show unto us the blessed fruit of thy womb, Jesus, O clement, O loving, O sweet Virgin Mary!

"*V*. Make me worthy to praise thee, holy Virgin.

"*R*. Give me strength against thine enemies.

"*V*. Blessed be God in His saints.

"*R*. Amen."

b. In the evening: "We fly to thy patronage, O holy Mother of God! Despise not our petitions in our necessities, and deliver us from all dangers, O ever glorious and blessed Virgin.

"Make me worthy, etc.," as above.

Indulgence of one hundred days once a day; seven years and seven quarantines on Sunday; two plenary indulgences each month on any two Sundays after confession, communion, and prayers for the Holy Father; a plenary indulgence on the same conditions on the feasts of the Blessed Virgin and all saints, also at the hour of death, and in the latter case if the person cannot receive the sacraments it is sufficient that he be sorry for his sins. These plenary indulgences are marked in their proper places farther on.

c. "My queen! my mother! remember I am thine own. Keep me, guard me, as thy property and possession."—Indulgence of forty days.

d. "To thee, O Virgin mother, never touched by stain of sin, actual or venial, I recommend and confide the purity of my heart."—One hundred days once a day.

e. "Mary, Mother of God and mother of mercy, pray for me and for the departed." —One hundred days once a day.

f. "Sweet heart of Mary, be my salvation!"—Three hundred days.

g. "Blessed be the holy and immaculate conception of the most blessed Virgin Mary, Mother of God."—Three hundred days.

h. "O Mary, who didst come into this world free from stain! obtain of God for me that I may leave it without sin."—One hundred days once a day.

i. "O Mary! conceived without sin, pray for us who have recourse to thee."—One hundred days once a day.

j. "Remember, O most gracious Virgin

Mary! that never was it known that any one who fled to thy protection, implored thy help, and sought thy intercession, was left unaided. Inspired with this confidence, I fly unto thee, O Virgin of virgins, my mother! To thee I come; before thee I stand, sinful and sorrowful. O Mother of the Word incarnate! despise not my petitions, but in thy mercy hear and answer me. Amen."—Three hundred days.

6. *Visiting an Image of the Blessed Virgin.*—Members of the archconfraternity of the Precious Blood of Jesus Christ can gain an indulgence of seven years and seven quarantines by visiting an image of the Blessed Virgin.

VI. THE HOLY FAMILY.

"Jesus, Mary, and Joseph, I give you my heart and my soul."

"Jesus, Mary, and Joseph, assist me in my last agony."

"Jesus, Mary, and Joseph, may I breathe forth my soul in peace with you."

One hundred days for each of these three ejaculations.

VII. THE GUARDIAN ANGEL.

"Angel of God, my guardian dear,
To whom His love commits me here,
Ever this day be at my side,
To light and guard, to rule and guide.
                    Amen."

One hundred days.

VIII. ST. JOSEPH.

1. "Remember, O most pure spouse of the Blessed Virgin Mary, my sweet protector St. Joseph! that no one ever had recourse to thy protection or implored thy aid without obtaining relief. Confiding therefore in thy goodness, I come before thee and humbly supplicate thee. Oh, despise not my petitions, foster-father of the Redeemer, but graciously receive them. Amen."—Three hundred days once a day.

2. "Guardian of virgins and father, holy Joseph, to whose faithful care Christ

Jesus, very innocent, and Mary, Virgin of virgins, were committed: I pray and beg of thee, by these dear pledges, Jesus and Mary, free me from all uncleanness, and make me, with spotless mind, pure heart, and chaste body, ever most chastely to serve Jesus and Mary all the days of my life. Amen."—One hundred days once a day.

3. "Help us, Joseph, in our early strife,
　E'er to lead a pure and blameless life."

Three hundred days, once a day.

4. "St. Joseph, model and patron of all those who love the Sacred Heart of Jesus, pray for us."

One hundred days once a day.

IX. PRAYER COMPOSED BY ST. THOMAS AQUINAS.

"Grant me grace, O merciful God, to desire ardently all that is pleasing to Thee, to examine it prudently, to acknowledge it truthfully, and to accomplish it perfectly, for the praise and glory of Thy name. Amen."

118 *Indulgences to be Gained Every Day.*

An indulgence of three hundred days to all the faithful who, before studying or reading, shall, with at least contrite heart and devotion, recite this prayer.

X. THE SOULS IN PURGATORY.

"Eternal rest give to them, O Lord, and may perpetual light shine upon them! May they rest in peace. Amen."

Two hundred days once a day.

XI. VARIOUS GOOD WORKS.

1. *Members of a Religious Confraternity* or pious organization gain from sixty to one hundred days' indulgence for every good work they perform.

2. *Meditation.*—*a.* The general indulgence attached to any pious exercise.

b. Blue Scapular of Immaculate Conception.—Sixty years if the wearer meditates for half an hour.

3. *Examen of Conscience in the Evening.*—*a.* The general indulgences attached to any pious exercise.

b. Sodalities of the Blessed Virgin.—Seven years and seven quarantines.

4. *Spiritual Canticles.*—The Sovereign Pontiff, Pius VII., in order to encourage the faithful to sing spiritual canticles, and to check, as far as possible, the singing of dangerous profane songs, granted an indulgence of one year, every time, to all who shall promote the singing of spiritual canticles, and an indulgence of one hundred days to all who, with at least contrite heart, shall practise this pious exercise.

5. *Act of Charity to Three Poor Persons.*—The Sovereign Pontiff Pius VII. granted to all the faithful who, being sorry for their sins, to honor Jesus, Mary, and Joseph, shall feed three poor persons, an indulgence of seven years and seven quarantines, and an indulgence of one hundred days to all the members of the family, or servants of those who do this charitable work, if they contribute to this work of mercy, either by lending their own services, or by their mere presence.

II. Indulgences which may be gained Every Week.

Plenary Indulgences.

1. *Members of the Association of the Communion of Reparation* who make this communion weekly.—Conditions: In addition to the communion, a visit to a church and prayers for the Holy Father's intentions are required.

2. *Daily Adorers of the Archconfraternity of the Sacred Heart of Jesus (Montmartre).*—Conditions: It must be gained on the day chosen for adoration, confession, communion, visit, prayers, and one hour of adoration.

3. *Apostleship of Prayer and League of the Sacred Heart of Jesus.*—*a.* For those members who practise the Holy Hour (that is, who present themselves, at least in spirit, before the Blessed Sacrament between sunset of Thursday and sunrise of Friday, and spend one hour either in

meditating upon the Passion of Our Lord, or in vocal prayer in union with His prayer in the Garden of Olives). Conditions: Confession, communion either Thursday or Friday, and the usual prayers.
b. Third Degree of the Apostleship. Conditions: Weekly communion of reparation, on the day appointed, if possible, preceded by confession, and, at any time during the day, a visit to a church, during which prayers must be offered for the Holy Father's intentions.

4. *Association of Prayer and Penance in Honor of the Sacred Heart of Jesus (Montmartre).*—The indulgence must be gained on the day chosen by the members, if possible. Conditions: Confession, communion, visit to a church, and the usual prayers.

5. *Sodalities of the Blessed Virgin.*—The indulgence is attached to the meeting-day of the sodalists, but may be gained on any other day of the week, if the meeting takes place on a week-day and the sodalists are unable to receive the sacraments on

that day. Conditions: Confession, communion, and the usual prayers, which should be recited during a visit to a church or chapel of the sodality.

6. *Wearers of the Red Scapular of the Sacred Passion* can gain a plenary indulgence every Friday. Conditions: Confession, communion, at least a short meditation on the Passion of Our Lord, and the usual prayers. In case of a lawful impediment, the indulgence can be gained on the following Sunday.

7. *Those who have made the Heroic Act of Charity* for the souls in purgatory can gain a plenary indulgence every Monday. Conditions: To assist at Mass on that day for the souls in purgatory, to visit a church, and to pray for the Sovereign Pontiff's intentions.

Partial Indulgences.

1. *For assisting at the Explanation of the Gospel* on Sunday in one's parish church.—Seven years each time.

2. *For assisting at any Sermon or Re-*

ligious *Exhortation.*—*a.* The general indulgence attached to any good work. *b.* Sodalities of the Blessed Virgin.—Seven years and seven quarantines. *c.* Blue Scapular of the Immaculate Conception.—Two hundred days.

3. *For assisting at the Divine Office sung in Choir.*—*a.* Indulgence attached to any good work. *b.* Sodalities of the Blessed Virgin.—Seven years and seven quarantines.

4. *Confession.*—*a.* Indulgence attached to any good work. *b.* Blue Scapular.—Seven years and seven quarantines.

III. Plenary Indulgences which may be gained Every Month.

A. Those attached to Special Days.

The First Sunday of the Month.

1. Archconfraternity of the Sacred Heart of Jesus (Rome).—Conditions: Confession, communion, and usual prayers.

N.B.—This indulgence may be gained on the first Friday of the month instead of the first Sunday.

2. Confraternity of the Holy Rosary.—Three plenary indulgences on the following respective conditions: *a.* Confession, communion in a confraternity church, and prayers for the Holy Father's intentions in the same church. *b.* Confession, communion, visit to an altar or chapel of the confraternity of the Rosary. *c.* Confession, communion, prayers, and participation in the monthly procession.

3. Blue Scapular of the Immaculate Conception.—Conditions: Confession, communion, participation in the procession, and prayers.

The First Thursday of the Month.

Association of Perpetual Adoration and Work for Poor Churches.—Conditions: Confession, communion, and the usual prayers during a visit to a church of the association.

The First Friday of the Month.

1. Association of Perpetual Adoration and Work for Poor Churches.—Conditions: Confession, communion, and prayers during a visit to a church of the association.

2. Archconfraternity of the Sacred Heart of Jesus (Rome).—Confession, communion, and prayers.

This indulgence can be gained on the first Sunday of the month instead of the first Friday.

The Third Sunday of the Month.

1. Confraternity of the Blessed Sacrament.—Conditions: Confession, communion, prayers during a visit to a church, and participation in the monthly procession.

2. Society of the Living Rosary.—Conditions: Confession, communion, and prayers during a visit to a church.

Last Sunday of the Month.

Those of the faithful who shall have recited, in company with others, five decades of the rosary at least three times a week for a month can gain a plenary indulgence on the last Sunday of the month. Conditions: Confession, communion, visit, and prayers.

The rosary used must be blessed and enriched with the Dominican indulgences.

B. Plenary Indulgences attached to Special Days of the Week in any Week chosen during the Month.

Sunday.

1. Confraternity of the Scapular of Our Lady of Mount Carmel.—Conditions: Confession, communion, prayers, and either participation in the procession or, if that is not possible, a visit to a church of the confraternity.

2. "Hail, holy queen," etc., and "We fly to thy patronage," etc. Those who recite these prayers every day, as prescribed on pages 112 and 113, can gain two plenary indulgences a month on two Sundays

chosen by themselves. Conditions for each: Confession, communion, and prayers.

Wednesday.

Archconfraternity of St. Joseph (Beauvais).—Two Wednesdays a month. Conditions: Confession, communion, visit, and prayers.

Friday.

Apostleship of Prayer.— Conditions: Confession, communion, and prayers during a visit to a church, which visit must be made between sunrise and sunset of the Friday chosen.

C. Plenary Indulgences attached to Days determined each Month by Circumstances of Place or Person.

1. *Archconfraternity of Perpetual Adoration and Work for Poor Churches.* — *a.* Day of the monthly meeting. Conditions: Confession, communion, prayers during a visit to a church of the

confraternity, assistance at Mass and at the instruction. *b.* Day on which the monthly hour of adoration is made. Conditions: Confession, communion, and prayers during a visit to a confraternity church.

2. *Association of the Communion of Reparation.*—(For those who make this communion only monthly.) Day appointed for receiving communion. Conditions: Communion, visit, and prayers.

3. *Archconfraternity of the Sacred Heart of Jesus (Montmartre).*—(For those who make their monthly adoration during the day.) Day appointed for the hour of adoration. Conditions: Confession, communion, visit, prayer, and hour of adoration.

4. *Apostleship of Prayer.*—*a.* Feast of the monthly patron marked on the leaflet which each member receives once a month. Conditions: Confession and communion. *b.* Third Degree of the Apostleship. Day appointed for the monthly communion of reparation. Conditions: Confession, communion, visit, and prayers. *c.* Third De-

gree of the Apostleship. Day appointed for the general communion. Conditions: Confession, communion, visit, and prayers.

5. *Association of Prayer and Penance in Honor of the Sacred Heart of Jesus (Montmartre).*—*a.* Members who devote one day every fortnight to prayer and penance can gain a plenary indulgence on each day so consecrated. Conditions: Confession, communion, visit, and prayers. *b.* Those who devote one day each month can gain a plenary indulgence on that day on the same conditions.

6. *Society for a Happy Death (Bona Mors Society).*—On the day of monthly meeting either on Friday or Sunday. Conditions: Confession, communion in a church of the society, and the customary prayers during exposition of the Blessed Sacrament.

Third Order of St. Francis.—Day of the monthly meeting. Conditions: Confession, communion, and prayers during a visit to a church.

Indulgences to be Gained Monthly.

D. Plenary Indulgences that can be gained Monthly on any Day selected by the Individual.

CONFRATERNITIES AND SCAPULARS.

1. *Association of Perpetual Adoration and Work for Poor Churches.*—a. Conditions: Confession, communion, and prayers during a visit to a church of the association. b. A second indulgence each month can be gained on the same conditions, but only by those who shall have spent six hours a week working for poor churches, and added some prayers to this work.

2. *Archconfraternity of the Precious Blood of Jesus Christ.*—Conditions: Confession, communion, and prayers during a visit to a church.

3. *Archconfraternity of the Sacred Heart of Jesus (Rome).*—Conditions: Confession, communion, and the usual prayers. Certain prayers must be recited every day for this indulgence (see page 52).

4. *Archconfraternity of the Sacred Heart of Jesus (Paray-le-Monial or Moulins).*—Conditions: Confession, communion, and prayers during a visit to a church of the confraternity.

5. *Archconfraternity of the Sacred Heart of Jesus (Montmartre).*—This indulgence is only for the zelators who make their adoration in the daytime. Conditions: Confession, communion, visit, prayer, and one hour of adoration.

6. *Archconfraternity of the Guard of Honor of the Sacred Heart of Jesus.*—Conditions: Confession, communion, and prayers during a visit to a church of the confraternity. It is also necessary to make the hour of guard every day according to the rules of the confraternity.

7. *Apostleship of Prayer.*—*a.* Conditions: Confession, communion, and prayers during a visit to a church. This visit must be made between sunrise and sunset of the day chosen. *b.* Promoters of the Apostleship can gain two indulgences each month on the feasts of their patrons. These

occur as follows: January 3d and 29th; February 1st and 13th; March 9th and 19th; April 5th and 30th; May 4th and 25th; June 3d and 29th; July 22d and 31st; August 4th and 21st; September 15th and 29th; October 4th and 15th; November 11th and 19th; December 13th and 27th. Conditions for these indulgences: Confession, communion of the promoters in a body, visit to a church, and prayers for the Holy Father's intentions.

8. *Association of Prayer and Penance in Honor of the Sacred Heart of Jesus* (*Montmartre*). — Zelators — Conditions: Confession, communion, visit, and prayers.

9. *Archconfraternity of Our Lady of the Sacred Heart.*—*a.* For those who recite the chaplet of Our Lady of the Sacred Heart every day. Conditions: Confession, communion, and prayers during a visit to a confraternity church. This visit can be made from the time for first vespers, that is, from two o'clock of the afternoon preceding the day chosen. *b.* Zelators—Con-

ditions: Confession, communion, and the usual prayers during a visit to their parish church.

10. *Archconfraternity of the Most Holy and Immaculate Heart of Mary for the Conversion of Sinners.* — Members can gain two plenary indulgences each month on days selected by themselves. Conditions· Confession, communion, and prayers during a visit to a church.

11. *Blue Scapular of the Immaculate Conception.*—*a.* Twice a month the wearers of this scapular can gain the plenary indulgence offered to those who visit the seven basilicas of Rome. This plenary indulgence may be gained from the first vespers to the sunset of the day selected. Conditions: Confession, communion, and prayers for the ordinary intentions before each of the seven altars in a church of the Theatine Fathers, or, where this is not possible, by visiting the altars of any church in which there is an altar of the Blessed Virgin seven times, and praying each time for the Pope's intentions.

b. Twice a month they can gain the indulgences attached to a visit to the holy sepulchre of Our Lord and the Holy Land. Conditions: Confession, communion, and the usual prayers during a visit to a church of the Theatine Fathers, or, if there is no such church in the place, to any church in which there is an altar of the Blessed Virgin.

12. *Society of the Holy Family.*—Conditions: Confession, communion, visit to the parish church, and the usual prayers. It is also necessary to recite every day the prayers prescribed for members of the association.

13. *Society for the Work of the Propagation of the Faith.*—Two plenary indulgences each month. Conditions: Confession, communion, and the usual prayers during a visit either to a church of the society or to the parish church.

14. *Third Order of St. Francis.*—*a.* Conditions: Confession, communion, and prayers during a visit to a church. *b.* Once a month members can gain the in-

dulgences of the stations of Rome, of the Portiuncula, of the holy places in the Holy Land, and of St. James in Compostella. Conditions: Confession, communion, and six Our Fathers and Hail Marys for the prescribed intentions.

Prayers and Devotions.

I. God and the Blessed Trinity.

1. *Glory be to the Father, etc.*—For those who recite this prayer morning, noon, and night each day for a month. Conditions: Confession, communion, and the usual prayers.

2. *Acts of Faith, Hope, and Charity.*—For those who recite these prayers every day for a month. Conditions: Confession, communion, and prayers.

II. Our Saviour Jesus Christ.

1. "O sweetest Heart of Jesus! I implore
 That I may ever love thee more and more."

For those who are accustomed to say this prayer every day during the month. Conditions: Confession, communion, and the usual prayers during a visit to a church.

   2. "O Sacrament most holy! O Sacrament divine!
     All praise and all thanksgiving be every moment thine."

For those who recite this prayer every day during the month. Conditions: Confession, communion, and prayers during a visit to a church.

   3. "Soul of Christ, sanctify me," etc. (see page 108).—For those who say this prayer every day during the month. Conditions: Confession, communion, and prayers during a visit to a church.

   4. "My Loving Jesus," etc. (see page 109).—For those who recite this prayer every day during the month before an image of the Sacred Heart of Jesus. Conditions: Confession, communion, and prayers.

III. THE BLESSED VIRGIN.

1. "Sweet heart of Mary, be my salvation!" For those who say this every day during the month. Conditions: Confession, communion, and prayers during a visit to a church.

2. The Angelus ("The Angel of the Lord," etc. See page 111).—For all the faithful who, every day, at the sound of the bell in the morning, or at noon, or in the evening, shall say this prayer in the proper manner. Conditions: Confession, communion, and prayers.

3. "Remember, O most gracious Virgin Mary," etc. (see page 114).—For those who say this prayer every day during the month. Conditions: Confession, communion, and prayers during a visit to a church.

IV. THE GUARDIAN ANGEL.

"Angel of God, my guardian dear," etc. (see page 116).—For those who say this prayer every day for a month. Conditions: Confession, communion, visit to a church, and prayers.

V. OTHER DEVOTIONS.

1. Mental Prayer or Meditation.

A plenary indulgence once a month for those who spend at least a quarter of an hour each day of the month at this devotion. Conditions: Confession, communion, and prayers.

2. Spiritual Canticles.

A plenary indulgence once a month for those who are accustomed to promote or practise the singing of spiritual canticles. Conditions: Confession, communion, and prayers.

B. Abridged List of Monthly Plenary Indulgences attached to certain Societies and Devotions.

Confraternity of the Blessed Sacrament.—One on the third Sunday of the month.

Association of Perpetual Adoration and Work for Poor Churches.—Six: 1. The first Thursday of the month; 2. The first Friday; 3. The day of the monthly meeting; 4. The day for monthly adoration; 5. Any other two days.

Association of the Communion of Reparation.—One on the day appointed for the communion.

Archconfraternity of the Precious Blood of Jesus Christ.—One on any day chosen by the individual members.

Archconfraternity of the Sacred Heart of Jesus (Rome).—Two: 1. Either the first Sunday or the first Friday; 2. One day to be selected by the member.

Archconfraternity of the Sacred Heart of Jesus (Moulins, Paray-le-Monial, or Montmartre).—Three: 1, 2. The two of the Roman archconfraternity; 3. Any other day selected by the members.

Archconfraternity of the Guard of Honor of the Sacred Heart of Jesus.—Three: 1, 2. Two the same as in the case of the Roman archconfraternity of the

Sacred Heart ; 3. Any other day chosen by the members.

Apostleship of Prayer.—Six: 1. Feast of the monthly patron; 2. Day of the communion of reparation ; 3. Day of the general communion; 4. One day to be chosen by the members ; 5, 6. Two special indulgences for Promoters of the League on the feasts of their patrons.

Archconfraternity of Our Lady of the Sacred Heart.—Two on days to be chosen by the members.

Confraternity of the Holy Rosary.—Four: 1-3. Three on the First Sunday ; 4. One on the last Sunday.

Society of the Living Rosary.—One on the third Sunday of the month.

Confraternity of the Scapular of Our Lady of Mount Carmel.—One on any Sunday at choice.

Archconfraternity of the Most Holy and Immaculate Heart of Mary for the Conversion of Sinners.—Two on any two days of the month.

Archconfraternity of St. Joseph (Beau-

vais).—Two on any two Wednesdays of the month.

Society of the Holy Family.—One on any day of the month.

Bona Mors Society.—One on the day of the monthly meeting.

Society for the Propagation of the Faith.—Two on any days selected.

Third Order of St. Francis.—Three : 1. On the day of the monthly meeting ; 2-3. Two on any two days selected.

Blue Scapular of the Immaculate Conception.—Five : 1. The first Sunday; 2-5. Four on any four days selected.

Prayers and Devotions.—Thirteen for the devotions mentioned on pages 135, 138 on any days chosen in the month.

IV. Plenary Indulgences which can be gained Every Year.

In the following calendar the day of the month or the feast is given first, then the name of the association or devotion to which the indulgence is attached, and finally the conditions for gaining the indulgence. In these conditions the word "prayers," as in the preceding sections of this chapter, denotes prayers for the intentions of the Sovereign Pontiff; "visit" means a visit to a church or public oratory. If the prayers must be said during the visit, or if the visit must be made to a particular church, these facts will be mentioned.

A. Days Determined According to the Different Months of the Year.

JANUARY.

1st. Circumcision of Our Lord.

Archconfraternity of the Precious Blood of Jesus Christ. Confession, communion, and visit.

Society of the Living Rosary. Confession, communion, and prayers during a visit.

Archconfraternity of the Most Holy and Immaculate Heart of Mary for the Conversion of Sinners. Confession and Communion.

Archconfraternity of St. Joseph (Rome and Beauvais). Confession, communion, visit, and prayers. In the Roman confraternity the visit may be made from first vespers.

Society of the Holy Family. Confession, communion, visit to the parish church, and prayers.

3d. St. Genevieve.

Promoters of the Apostleship of Prayer. Confession, communion, visit, and prayers.

6th. Epiphany.

Archconfraternity of the Precious Blood of Jesus Christ. Confession, communion, and visit. This indulgence may be gained either on the feast or any day during the octave.

Archconfraternity of the Sacred Heart of Jesus (Montmartre). For the adorers who make their adoration during the day. Confession, communion, visit, prayers, and one hour of adoration.

144 *Indulgences to be Gained in January.*

Archconfraternity of Our Lady of the Sacred Heart. Confession, communion, and prayers during a visit to a church of the confraternity. The visit may be made from the time for first vespers.

Society of the Living Rosary. Confession, communion, and prayers during a visit.

Archconfraternity of St. Joseph (Rome and Beauvais). Confession, communion, visit, and prayers. The visit may be made from first vespers in the case of the Roman confraternity.

Society of the Holy Family. Confession, communion, visit to the parish church, and prayers.

Archconfraternity of the Holy Family (Liège). Confession, communion, visit to the confraternity or parish church, and prayers. This indulgence may be gained during the octave, and the visit may be made from first vespers of the day selected.

Bona Mors Society. Confession, communion in a church of the society, and prayers.

Society for the Propagation of the Faith. Confession, communion, and prayers during a visit to the confraternity or parish church.

Blue Scapular of the Immaculate Conception. Confession, communion, visit, and prayers.

Scapular of St. Joseph. Confession, communion, and prayers during a visit, which may be made from first vespers.

Apostolic Indulgences (for those who have objects enriched with these indulgences in their possession and comply with the devotional rules prescribed; see page 79). Confession, communion, and prayers.

Sermon (for those who are accustomed to assist at the explanation of the Gospel on all the Sundays of the year in the parish church). Confession and communion.

23d. *The Espousals of the Blessed Virgin and St. Joseph.*

Archconfraternity of St. Joseph (Rome and Beauvais). Confession, communion, visit, and prayers. In the Roman confraternity the visit may be made from the time for first vespers.

Archconfraternity of St. Joseph (Angers). Confession, communion, and prayers during a visit to a church of the confraternity. The visit may be made from first vespers.

Society of the Holy Family. Confession, communion, visit to the parish church, and prayers.

25*th.* Conversion of St. Paul.

Archconfraternity of the Most Holy and Immaculate Heart of Mary for the Conversion of Sinners. Confession and communion.

29*th.* St. Francis de Sales.

Promoters of the Apostleship of Prayer. Confession, communion, visit, and prayers.

FEBRUARY.

1*st.* St. Ignatius (*Martyr*).

Promoters of the Apostleship of Prayer. Confession, communion, visit, and prayers.

2d. Purification of the Blessed Virgin.

Association of Perpetual Adoration and Work for Poor Churches. Confession, communion, and prayers during a visit to a church of the confraternity.

Archconfraternity of the Precious Blood of Jesus Christ. Confession, communion, and visit to a church of the confraternity.

Archconfraternity of the Sacred Heart of Jesus (Rome). Confession, communion, and a visit to a church of the confraternity.

Archconfraternity of Our Lady of the Sacred Heart. Confession, communion, and prayers during a visit to a church of the confraternity. This visit may be made from first vespers.

Confraternity of the Holy Rosary. (Five indulgences.)

1. Visit to a chapel of the rosary from first vespers.

2. Confession, communion, and prayers during a visit.

3. Confession, communion, visit to a chapel of the rosary, and prayers.

4. Confession, communion, and visit to a church of the confraternity.

5. Procession.

Society of the Living Rosary. Confession, communion, and prayers during a visit.

Confraternity of the Scapular of Our Lady of Mount Carmel. Confession, communion, and prayers during a visit to the confraternity or parish church.

Sodalities of the Blessed Virgin. Confession and communion.

Archconfraternity of the Most Holy and Immaculate Heart of Mary for the Conversion of Sinners. Confession and communion.

Archconfraternity of St. Joseph (Rome and Beauvais). Confession, communion, visit, and prayers. In the case of the Roman confraternity the visit may be made from first vespers.

Archconfraternity of St. Joseph (Angers). Confession, communion, and prayers during a visit to a confraternity church. The visit may be made from first vespers.

Society of the Holy Family. Confession, communion, visit to the parish church, and prayers.

Archconfraternity of the Holy Family (Liège). Confession, communion, visit to a confraternity or parish church, and prayers. This indulgence may be gained during the octave.

Bona Mors Society. Confession, communion in a church of the confraternity, and prayers.

Blue Scapular of the Immaculate Conception. Confession, communion, visit, and prayers.

Scapular of St. Joseph. Confession, communion, and prayers during a visit, which may be made from first vespers.

Apostolic Indulgences. Confession, communion, and prayers.

Litany of the Blessed Virgin (for those who recite it every day). Confession, communion, and prayers during a visit.

"Hail, holy queen," etc., and "We fly to thy patronage," etc. (pages 112, 113; for those who say these prayers daily as directed). Confession, communion, and prayers.

4th. *St. Andrew Corsini.*

Confraternity of the Scapular of Our Lady of Mount Carmel. Confession, communion, and prayers during a visit to the parish or confraternity church.

13th. *St. Catherine de Ricci.*

Promoters of the Apostleship of Prayer. Confession, communion, visit, and prayers.

17th. *Flight of Our Lord into Egypt.*

Archconfraternity of the Holy Family (Liège). Confession, communion, visit to the parish or confraternity church, and prayers.

N.B.—The visit may be made from first vespers and the indulgence may be gained during the octave.

24th. *St. Matthias, Apostle.*

Archconfraternity of St. Joseph (Beauvais). Confession, communion, visit, and prayers.

Society for the Propagation of the Faith. Confession, communion, and prayers during a visit to the parish or confraternity church.

Bona Mors Society. Confession, communion in a church of the confraternity, and prayers.

Apostolic Indulgences. Confession, communion, and prayers.

Association of Perpetual Adoration and Work for Poor Churches. Confession, communion, and prayers during a visit to a church of the association.

MARCH.

Month of St. Joseph.

Those who perform any act of devotion, on each day of the month of March, in honor of St. Joseph can gain—

1. An indulgence of three hundred days each day.

2. A plenary indulgence on any one day of the month. Conditions: Confession, communion, and prayers.

152 *Indulgences to be Gained in March.*

And these indulgences can be gained also if the devotion is begun so as to finish the thirty-one days on the feast of St. Joseph, March 19th.

3. Members of the Archconfraternity of the Precious Blood of Jesus Christ who practise this devotion can gain a plenary indulgence every Friday of the month. Conditions: Confession, communion, and visit.

4. Members of the Archconfraternity of St. Joseph (Beauvais) practising this devotion can gain a plenary indulgence every Wednesday of the month. Confession, communion, visit, and prayers.

9th. St. Frances of Rome.

Promoters of the Apostleship of Prayer. Confession, communion, visit, and prayers.

12th. St. Gregory the Great.

Archconfraternity of the Sacred Heart of Jesus (Rome). Confession, communion, and prayers during a visit to a confraternity church.

Indulgences to be Gained in March. 153

18*th. St. Gabriel, Archangel.*

Archconfraternity of the Holy Family (Liège). Confession, communion, visit from first vespers to the parish or confraternity church, and prayers. This indulgence may be gained during the octave.

19*th. St. Joseph.*

Promoters of the Apostleship of Prayer. Confession, communion, visit, and prayers.

Archconfraternity of the Precious Blood of Jesus Christ. Confession, communion, and visit.

Archconfraternity of the Sacred Heart of Jesus (Rome). Confession, communion, and visit to a church of the confraternity.

Archconfraternity of the Most Holy and Immaculate Heart of Mary for the Conversion of Sinners. Confession, communion, and prayers.

Confraternity of the Scapular of Our Lady of Mount Carmel. Confession, communion, and prayers during a visit to a confraternity or parish church.

Archconfraternity of St. Joseph (Rome

and Beauvais). Confession, communion, visit (in the Roman confraternity from first vespers), and prayers.

Archconfraternity of St. Joseph (Angers). Confession, communion, and prayers during a visit to a confraternity church. The visit may be made from first vespers.

Society of the Holy Family. Confession, communion, visit to the parish church, and prayers.

Archconfraternity of the Holy Family (Liège). Confession, communion, visit from first vespers to a confraternity or parish church, and prayers. The indulgence may be gained during the octave.

Bona Mors Society. Confession, communion in a confraternity church, and prayers.

Third Order of St. Francis. Members are entitled on this feast to the general absolution, or a blessing to which is attached a plenary indulgence. This blessing, if given privately in the confessional, may be received from first vespers. Confession, communion, and prayers.

Indulgences to be Gained in March. 155

Blue Scapular of the Immaculate Conception. Confession, communion, visit, and prayers.

Scapular of St. Joseph. Confession, communion, visit from first vespers, and prayers.

Apostolic Indulgences. Confession, communion, and prayers.

24th. *Vigil of the Annunciation.*

Blue Scapular of the Immaculate Conception. Confession, communion, visit, and prayers.

25th. *Annunciation.*

Association of Perpetual Adoration and Work for Poor Churches. Confession, communion, and prayers during a visit to a church of the confraternity.

Archconfraternity of the Precious Blood of Jesus Christ. Confession, communion, and visit.

Archconfraternity of the Sacred Heart

of Jesus (Rome). Confession, communion, and a visit to a church of the confraternity.

Archconfraternity of Our Lady of the Sacred Heart. Confession, communion, and prayers during a visit from first vespers to a church of the confraternity.

Confraternity of the Holy Rosary. (Six indulgences.)

1. Visit to a chapel of the rosary from first vespers.
2. Confession, communion, and prayers during a visit.
3. Confession, communion, visit to a chapel of the rosary, and prayers.
4. Procession.
5. Confession, communion, and a visit to a confraternity church.
6. Confession, communion, and the recital of the rosary.

Society of the Living Rosary. Confession, communion, and prayers during a visit.

Confraternity of the Scapular of Our Lady of Mount Carmel. Confession, communion, and prayers during a visit to the parish or confraternity church.

Sodalities of the Blessed Virgin. Confession and communion.

Archconfraternity of the Most Holy and Immaculate Heart of Mary for the Conversion of Sinners. Confession and communion.

Archconfraternity of St. Joseph (Rome and Beauvais). Confession, communion, visit, and prayers. In the Roman confraternity the visit may be made from first vespers.

Archconfraternity of St. Joseph (Angers). Confession, communion, and prayers during a visit from first vespers to a church of the confraternity.

Society of the Holy Family. Confession, communion, visit to the parish church, and prayers.

Bona Mors Society. Confession, communion in a church of the confraternity, and prayers.

Society for the Propagation of the Faith. Confession, communion, and prayers during a visit to the confraternity or parish church. This indulgence may be gained during the octave.

Blue Scapular of the Immaculate Conception. Confession, communion, visit, and prayers.

Scapular of St. Joseph. Confession, communion, and prayers during a visit from first vespers.

Apostolic Indulgences. Confession, communion, and prayers.

Litany of the Blessed Virgin (every day). Confession, communion, and prayers during a visit.

"Hail, holy queen," etc., and "We fly to thy patronage," etc. Confession, communion, and prayers.

28th.

Archconfraternity of the Precious Blood of Jesus Christ. Confession, communion, and visit.

APRIL.

4th. St. Isidore, Bishop and Doctor.

Association of Perpetual Adoration and Work for Poor Churches. Confession, communion, and prayers during a visit to a church of the association.

5th. *St. Vincent Ferrer.*

Promoters of the Apostleship of Prayer. Confession, communion, visit, and prayers.

5th. *St. Juliana de Cornillon.*

Association of Perpetual Adoration and Work for Poor Churches. Confession, communion, and prayers during a visit to a confraternity church.

Archconfraternity of the Holy Family (Liège). Confession, communion, visit to the parish or confraternity church, and prayers. The visit may be made from first vespers and the indulgence may be gained during the octave.

Sunday following the 7th of April.

Archconfraternity of the Holy Family. (Liège). Confession, communion, visit from first vespers to the parish or confraternity church, and prayers. The indulgence may be gained during the octave.

160 *Indulgences to be Gained in April.*

12th. St. Julius, Pope.

Blue Scapular of the Immaculate Conception. Confession, communion, visit, and prayers.

16th. St. Benedict Labre.

Association of Prayer and Penance in Honor of the Sacred Heart of Jesus (Montmartre). Confession, communion, visit, and prayers.

Third Sunday.

Confraternity of the Holy Rosary. Confession, communion, visit to an altar of the rosary, and prayers.

23d. St. George.

Archconfraternity of the Holy Family (Liège). Confession, communion, visit from first vespers to a parish or confraternity church, and prayers.

This indulgence may be gained during the octave.

30*th. St. Catherine of Sienna.*

Promoters of the Apostleship of Prayer. Confession, communion, visit, and prayers.

MAY.

Month of Mary.

Those who honor the Blessed Virgin by some special prayers or act of virtue every day of the month can gain—

1. Three hundred days' indulgence every day.

2. Plenary indulgence on any one day of the month. Conditions for plenary indulgence: Confession, communion, and prayers.

1*st. St. Philip and St. James, Apostles.*

Archconfraternity of St. Joseph (Beauvais). Confession, communion, visit, and prayers.

Bona Mors Society. Confession, communion in a church of the society, and prayers.

162 Indulgences to be Gained in May.

Society for the Propagation of the Faith. Confession, communion, and prayers during a visit to the parish or confraternity church.

Apostolic Indulgences. Confession, communion, and prayers.

3d. Finding of the Holy Cross.

Archconfraternity of the Precious Blood of Jesus Christ. Confession, communion, and visit.

Society for the Propagation of the Faith. Confession, communion, and prayers during a visit to the parish or confraternity church. This indulgence may be gained during the octave.

Blue Scapular of the Immaculate Conception. Confession, communion, visit, and prayers.

4th. St. Monica.

Promoters of the Apostleship of Prayer. Confession, communion, visit, and prayers.

5th. St. Pius V.

Archconfraternity of the Sacred Heart of Jesus (Rome). Confession, communion, and prayers during a visit to a church of the confraternity. The visit may be made from first vespers.

5th St. Angelus, a Carmelite Friar.

Confraternity of the Scapular of Our Lady of Mount Carmel. Confession, communion, and prayers during a visit to the confraternity or parish church.

16th. St. Simon Stock.

Confraternity of the Scapular of Our Lady of Mount Carmel. Confession, communion, and prayers during a visit to the confraternity or parish church.

24th. Our Lady, Help of Christians.

Archconfraternity of the Precious Blood of Jesus Christ. Confession, communion, and visit. This indulgence may be gained during the octave.

Indulgences to be Gained in June.

25th. St. Mary Magdalen de Pazzi.

Confraternity of the Scapular of Our Lady of Mount Carmel. Confession, communion, and prayers during a visit to the confraternity or parish church.

25th. St. Gregory VII.

Promoters of the Apostleship of Prayer. Confession, communion, visit, and prayers.

31st. Our Lady of the Sacred Heart.

Archconfraternity of Our Lady of the Sacred Heart. Confession, communion, and prayers during a visit from first vespers to a church of the confraternity. This indulgence may be gained during the octave.

JUNE.

Month of the Sacred Heart.

Those who practise any special devotions every day of the month in honor of the Sacred Heart can gain the following indulgences:

1. Seven years and seven quarantines every day.

2. A plenary indulgence any one day of the month. Confession, communion, and prayers during a visit.

3d. *St. Clotilda.*

Promoters of the Apostleship of Prayer. Confession, communion, visit, and prayers.

Archconfraternity of the Sacred Heart of Jesus (Montmartre). Members who make their adoration during the day are offered a plenary indulgence on the feast of St. Clotilda, but have the privilege of being able to gain it on any other day of the month. Confession, communion, visit, prayers, and an hour of adoration.

Association of Prayer and Penance in honor of the Sacred Heart of Jesus. Confession, communion, visit, and prayers.

14th. *St. Eliseus, Prophet.*

Confraternity of the Scapular of Our Lady of Mount Carmel. Confession, communion, and prayers during a visit to the parish or confraternity church.

17th. *St. Botulph.*

Blue Scapular of the Immaculate Conception. Confession, communion, visit, and prayers.

24th. *St. John the Baptist.*

Association of Perpetual Adoration and Work for Poor Churches. Confession, communion, and prayers during a visit to a confraternity church.

Archconfraternity of the Precious Blood of Jesus Christ. Confession, communion, and visit.

Archconfraternity of the Most Holy and Immaculate Heart of Mary for the Conversion of Sinners. Confession, communion, and prayers.

Bona Mors Society. Confession, communion in a confraternity church, and prayers.

Blue Scapular of the Immaculate Conception. Confession, communion, visit, and prayers.

Apostolic Indulgences. Confession, communion, and prayers.

29th. St. Peter and St. Paul.

Promoters of the Apostleship of Prayer. Confession, communion, visit, and prayers.

Association of Perpetual Adoration and Work for Poor Churches. Confession, communion, and prayers during a visit to a church of the association.

Archconfraternity of the Holy Face. Confession, communion, and prayers during a visit to a church of the confraternity. This indulgence may be gained during the octave.

Archconfraternity of the Precious Blood of Jesus Christ. Confession, communion, and visit. This indulgence may be gained during the octave.

Archconfraternity of the Sacred Heart of Jesus (Rome). Confession, communion, and visit to a church of the confraternity.

Association of Prayer and Penance in

honor of the Sacred Heart of Jesus (Montmartre). Confession, communion, visit, and prayers.

Society of the Living Rosary. Confession, communion, and prayers during a visit.

Archconfraternity of St. Joseph (Beauvais). Confession, communion, visit, and prayers.

Archconfraternity of the Holy Family (Liège). Confession, communion, visit from first vespers to the parish or confraternity church, and prayers. This indulgence may be gained during the octave.

Bona Mors Society. Confession, communion in a church of the confraternity, and prayers.

Society for the Propagation of the Faith. Confession, communion, and prayers during a visit to the parish or confraternity church.

Blue Scapular of the Immaculate Conception. Confession, communion, visit, and prayers.

Apostolic Indulgences. Confession, communion, and prayers. Attendance at the explanation of the Gospel on all the Sundays of the year. Confession and communion.

JULY.

First Sunday: Feast of the Precious Blood of Jesus Christ.

Archconfraternity of the Precious Blood of Jesus Christ. Confession, communion, and visit. This indulgence may be gained during the octave.

Archconfraternity of the Holy Family (Liège). Confession, communion, visit from first vespers to the parish or confraternity church, and prayers. This indulgence can be gained during the octave.

Third Sunday (or in some places October 23d). Most Holy Redeemer.

Archconfraternity of the Precious Blood of Jesus Christ. Confession, communion, and visit.

Archconfraternity of the Holy Family (Liège). Confession, communion, visit from first vespers to the parish or confraternity church, and prayers. It may be gained during the octave.

Last Sunday.

Blue Scapular of the Immaculate Conception. Confession, communion, visit, and prayers.

2d. *Feast of the Visitation of the Blessed Virgin.*

Confraternity of the Holy Rosary. (Four indulgences.)

1. Visit to a chapel of the rosary from first vespers.
2. Confession, communion, and prayers during a visit.
3. Procession.
4. Confession, communion, and a visit to a chapel of the rosary.

Society of the Living Rosary. Confession, communion, and prayers during a visit.

Indulgences to be Gained in July. 171

Confraternity of the Scapular of Our Lady of Mount Carmel. Confession, communion, and prayers during a visit to the parish or confraternity church.

Archconfraternity of the Most Holy and Immaculate Heart of Mary for the Conversion of Sinners. Confession and communion.

Archconfraternity of St. Joseph (Rome). Confession, communion, visit from first vespers, and prayers.

Archconfraternity of St. Joseph (Angers). Confession, communion, and prayers during a visit from first vespers to a church of the confraternity.

Sunday following July 13*th.*

Association of Perpetual Adoration and Work for Poor Churches. Confession, communion, and prayers during a visit to a church of the confraternity.

14*th. St. Bonaventure.*

Archconfraternity of St. Joseph (Beauvais). Confession, communion, visit to a church of the confraternity, and prayers. Members may gain this indulgence on the Sunday preceding or following the feast.

16th. Our Lady of Mount Carmel.

From first vespers of this feast all the faithful can gain a plenary indulgence every time they visit and pray devoutly in a church of the Carmelites. The other conditions are: Confession and communion.

Archconfraternity of the Precious Blood of Jesus Christ. Confession, communion, and visit.

Society of the Living Rosary. Confession, communion, and prayers during a visit.

Confraternity of the Scapular of Our Lady of Mount Carmel. Confession, communion, and prayers. This indulgence may be gained on the following Sunday instead, and in some places on any Sunday of the month.

20th. *St. Elias, Prophet.*

Confraternity of the Scapular of Our Lady of Mount Carmel. Confession, communion, and prayers during a visit to the confraternity or parish church.

20th. *St. Jerome Emilian.*

For those who recite every day for a year the prayer, "My sweetest Jesus, be not my Judge, but my Saviour." Confession, communion, and prayers during a visit, which may be made from first vespers. This indulgence can be gained during the octave.

22d. *St. Mary Magdalen.*

Promoters of the Apostleship of Prayer. Confession, communion, visit, and prayers.

Association of Perpetual Adoration and Work for Poor Churches. Confession, communion, and prayers during a visit to a church of the confraternity.

Association of Prayer and Penance in

honor of the Sacred Heart of Jesus. Confession, communion, visit, and prayers.

Archconfraternity of the Most Holy and Immaculate Heart of Mary for the Conversion of Sinners. Confession and communion.

25th. St. James, Apostle.

Archconfraternity of St. Joseph (Beauvais). Confession, communion, visit, and prayers.

Bona Mors Society. Confession, communion in a church of the society, and prayers.

Society for the Propagation of the Faith. Confession, communion, and prayers during a visit to the confraternity or parish church.

Apostolic Indulgences. Confession, communion, and prayers.

26th. St. Anne.

Archconfraternity of the Sacred Heart of Jesus (Montmartre). Confession, communion, and prayers during a visit from first vespers to the parish church.

Confraternity of the Scapular of Our Lady of Mount Carmel. Confession, communion, and prayers during a visit to the confraternity or parish church.

Archconfraternity of the Holy Family (Liège). Confession, communion, visit from first vespers to the confraternity or parish church, and prayers. This indulgence may be gained during the octave.

29th. St. Martha.

Association of Perpetual Adoration and Work for Poor Churches. Confession, communion, and prayers during a visit to a church of the confraternity.

31st. St. Ignatius Loyola.

Promoters of the Apostleship of Prayer. Confession, communion, visit, and prayers.

Association of Perpetual Adoration and Work for Poor Churches. Confession, communion, and prayers during a visit to a church of the confraternity.

AUGUST.

2d. Portiuncula.

All the faithful can gain a plenary indulgence as often as they visit devoutly a church of the Franciscan Fathers, or any church to which the same privilege has been extended.

The conditions are confession, communion, and prayers. The visits may be made from first vespers, and the confession may be made as early as July 30th. It is not necessary to receive communion in a Franciscan church.

2d. Feast of Our Lady of the Angels.

Third Order of St. Francis. Confession and communion.

Blue Scapular of the Immaculate Conception. Confession, communion, visit, and prayers.

2d. St. Alphonsus Liguori.

Archconfraternity of the Holy Family (Liège). Confession, communion, visit

from first vespers to the parish or confraternity church, and prayers. This indulgence can be gained during the octave.

4th. St. Dominic.

Promoters of the League of the Sacred Heart. Confession, communion, visit, and prayers.

5th. Our Lady of the Snows.

Society of the Living Rosary. Confession, communion, and prayers during a visit.

6th. The Transfiguration of Our Lord.

Archconfraternity of the Holy Face. Confession, communion, and prayers during a visit to a church of the confraternity. This indulgence may be gained during the octave.

7th. St. Cajetan.

Blue Scapular of the Immaculate Conception. Confession communion, visit, and prayers.

7th. St. Albert.

Confraternity of the Scapular of Our Lady of Mount Carmel. Confession, communion, and prayers during a visit to the parish or confraternity church.

12th. St. Clare.

Third Order of St. Francis. Confession and communion.

15th. *Assumption of the Blessed Virgin.*

Association of Perpetual Adoration and Work for Poor Churches. Confession, communion, and prayers during a visit to a confraternity church.

Archconfraternity of the Precious Blood of Jesus Christ. Confession, communion, and visit. This indulgence may be gained during the octave.

Archconfraternity of the Sacred Heart of Jesus (Rome). Confession, communion, and visit to a church of the confraternity.

Archconfraternity of Our Lady of the Sacred Heart. Confession, communion, and prayers during a visit from first vespers to a church of the confraternity.

Confraternity of the Holy Rosary. (Five indulgences.)

1. Visit to a chapel of the rosary. This visit may be made from first vespers.

2. Confession, communion, visit to a chapel of the rosary, and prayers.

3. Procession.

4. Confession, communion, visit from first vespers to a church of the society, and prayers.

5. Confession, communion, and a visit to a chapel of the rosary.

Society of the Living Rosary. Confession, communion, and prayers during a visit.

Confraternity of the Scapular of Our Lady of Mount Carmel. Confession, communion, and prayers during a visit to the parish or confraternity church.

Sodalities of the Blessed Virgin. Confession and communion.

Archconfraternity of the Most Holy and Immaculate Heart of Mary for the

Conversion of Sinners. Confession and communion.

Archconfraternity of St. Joseph (Rome and Beauvais). Confession, communion, visits, and prayers. In the Roman confraternity the visit may be made from first vespers.

Archconfraternity of St. Joseph (Angers). Confession, communion, and prayers during a visit from first vespers to a confraternity church.

Society of the Holy Family. Confession, communion, visit to the parish church, and prayers.

Archconfraternity of the Holy Family (Liège). Confession, communion, visit from first vespers to the confraternity or parish church. This indulgence may be gained during the octave.

Bona Mors Society. Confession, communion in a church of the society, and prayers.

Society for the Propagation of the Faith. Confession, communion, and prayers during a visit to the confraternity

Indulgences to be Gained in August. 181

or parish church. This indulgence may be gained during the octave.

Blue Scapular of the Immaculate Conception. Confession, communion, visit, and prayers.

Scapular of St. Joseph. Confession, communion, and prayers during a visit, which may be made from first vespers.

Apostolic Indulgences. Confession, communion, and prayers.

Litany of the Blessed Virgin. Confession, communion, and prayers during a visit

"Hail, holy queen," etc., and "We fly to thy patronage," etc. Confession, communion, and prayers.

Sunday following the Assumption: St. Joachim.

Confraternity of the Scapular of Our Lady of Mount Carmel. Confession, communion, and prayers during a visit to the confraternity or parish church.

Archconfraternity of the Holy Family (Liège). Confession, communion, visit

from first vespers to the parish or confraternity church, and prayers. This indulgence may be gained during the octave.

Sunday following the Octave of the Assumption: Most Pure Heart of Mary.

Association of Perpetual Adoration and Work for Poor Churches. Confession, communion, and prayers during a visit to a church of the confraternity.

Apostleship of Prayer—Members of Second Degree. Confession, communion, and prayers during a visit to the confraternity or parish church.

Archconfraternity of the Holy Family (Liège). Confession, communion, visit from first vespers to the confraternity or parish church, and prayers. This indulgence may be gained during the octave.

21st. St. Jane Frances de Chantal.

Promoters of the Apostleship of Prayer. Confession, communion, visit, and prayers.

24th. St. Bartholomew, Apostle.

Confraternity of the Scapular of Our Lady of Mount Carmel. Confession, communion, and prayers during a visit from first vespers to a church of the confraternity.

Archconfraternity of St. Joseph (Beauvais). Confession, communion, visit, and prayers.

Bona Mors Society. Confession, communion in a church of the association, and prayers.

Society for the Propagation of the Faith. Confession, communion, and prayers during a visit to the confraternity or parish church.

Apostolic Indulgences. Confession, communion, and prayers.

25th. St. Louis.

Archconfraternity of the Sacred Heart of Jesus (Montmartre). Confession, communion, and prayers during a visit from first vespers to the parish church.

Third Order of St. Francis. General absolution may be received from first vespers. Confession, communion, and prayers.

27th.

Confraternity of the Scapular of Our Lady of Mount Carmel. Confession, communion, and prayers during a visit to the confraternity or parish church.

28th. *St. Augustine.*

Archconfraternity of the Most Holy and Immaculate Heart of Mary for the Conversion of Sinners. Confession and communion.

Blue Scapular of the Immaculate Conception. Confession, communion, visit, and prayers.

SEPTEMBER.

Third Sunday: Seven Sorrows of the Blessed Virgin Mary.

Archconfraternity of the Precious Blood of Jesus Christ. Confession, communion, and visit.

Society of the Living Rosary. Confession, communion, and prayers during a visit.

Archconfraternity of the Holy Family (Liège). Confession, communion, visit from first vespers to the parish or confraternity church, and prayers. This indulgence may be gained during the octave.

Bona Mors Society. Confession, communion, and prayers during a visit from first vespers to a church of the confraternity.

8th. *Birth of the Blessed Virgin.*

Association of Perpetual Adoration and Work for Poor Churches. Confession, communion, and prayers during a visit to a confraternity church.

Archconfraternity of the Precious Blood of Jesus Christ. Confession, communion, visit.

Archconfraternity of the Sacred Heart of Jesus (Rome). Confession, communion, and visit to a church of the confraternity.

Archconfraternity of Our Lady of the

Sacred Heart. Confession, communion, and prayers during a visit from first vespers to a church of the confraternity.

Confraternity of the Holy Rosary. (Four indulgences.)

1. Visit to a chapel of the rosary from the time for first vespers.
2. Confession, communion, and prayers during a visit.
3. Confession, communion, visit to a chapel of the rosary, and prayers.
4. Procession.

Society of the Living Rosary. Confession, communion, and prayers during a visit.

Confraternity of the Scapular of Our Lady of Mount Carmel. Confession, communion, and prayers during a visit to the parish or confraternity church.

Sodalities of the Blessed Virgin. Confession and communion.

Archconfraternity of the Most Holy and Immaculate Heart of Mary for the Conversion of Sinners. Confession and communion.

Archconfraternity of St. Joseph (Rome

and Beauvais). Confession, communion, visit, and prayer. The visit may be made from first vespers in the Roman confraternity.

Archconfraternity of St. Joseph (Angers). Confession, communion, and prayers during a visit from first vespers to a church of the confraternity.

Society of the Holy Family. Confession, communion, visit to the parish church, and prayers.

Archconfraternity of the Holy Family (Liège). Confession, communion, visit from first vespers to the parish or confraternity church, and prayers. This indulgence may be gained during the octave.

Bona Mors Society. Confession, communion in a church of the confraternity, and prayers.

Blue Scapular of the Immaculate Conception. Confession, communion, visit, and prayers.

Scapular of St. Joseph. Confession, communion, and prayers during a visit, which may be made from first vespers.

Apostolic Indulgences. Confession, communion, and prayers.

Litany of the Blessed Virgin (every day). Confession, communion, and prayers during a visit.

"Hail, holy queen," etc., and "We fly to thy patronage," etc. (every day). Confession, communion, and prayers.

Sunday within the Octave: Holy Name of Mary.

Confraternity of the Holy Rosary. Confession, communion, visit to an altar of the rosary, and prayers.

Society of the Living Rosary. Confession, communion, and prayers during a visit.

14*th. Exaltation of the Holy Cross.*

Archconfraternity of the Precious Blood of Jesus Christ. Confession, communion, and prayers.

Archconfraternity of the Holy Family (Liège). Confession, communion, visit from first vespers to the confraternity or parish church, and prayers. This indulgence can be gained during the octave.

Blue Scapular of the Immaculate Conception. Confession, communion, visit, and prayers.

15th. St. Catherine of Genoa.

Promoters of the Apostleship of Prayer. Confession, communion, visit, and prayers.

17th. Stigmata of St. Francis of Assisi.

Third Order of St. Francis. Members can receive the general absolution from first vespers. Confession, communion, and prayers.

21st. St. Matthew, Apostle.

Archconfraternity of St. Joseph (Beauvais). Confession, communion, visit, and prayers.

Bona Mors Society. Confession, communion in a church of the confraternity, and prayers.

Society for the Propagation of the Faith. Confession, communion, and prayers during a visit to the parish or confraternity church.

Apostolic Indulgences. Confession, communion, and prayers.

24th. *Our Lady of Mercy (or Ransom)*.

Society of the Living Rosary. Confession, communion, and prayers during a visit.

29th. *St. Michael, Archangel*.

Archconfraternity of the Sacred Heart of Jesus (Montmartre). Confession, communion, and prayers during a visit from first vespers to the parish church.

Promoters of the Apostleship of Prayer Confession, communion, visit, and prayers.

Archconfraternity of the Holy Family. (Liège). Confession, communion, visit from first vespers to the parish or confraternity church, and prayers. This indulgence may be gained during the octave.

Society for the Propagation of the Faith. Confession, communion, and prayers during a visit to the parish or confraternity church.

Blue Scapular of the Immaculate Conception. Confession, communion, visit, and prayers.

OCTOBER.

Month of the Holy Rosary.

1. Seven years and seven quarantines each day for those who recite the rosary regularly during the month.

2. A plenary indulgence on any day at choice for those who assist at the public recital of the rosary and prescribed prayers at least ten times during the month, or, in case of legitimate impediment, say these prayers at home.

First Sunday: Feast of the Holy Rosary. All those who go to confession and communion in memory of the Christian victory at Lepanto over the Turks can gain a plenary indulgence every time they visit a chapel of the rosary and pray there for the intentions of the Holy Father.

These visits may commence from first vespers.

Archconfraternity of the Precious Blood of Jesus Christ. Confession, communion, and visit. This indulgence can be gained during the octave.

Confraternity of the Holy Rosary. Confession, communion, and visit to a church of the confraternity. This is in addition to the regular indulgences granted to members on the first Sunday of every month.

Society of the Living Rosary. Confession, communion, and prayers during a visit.

Devout assistance at the public exercises at least ten times during the month. Confession, communion, and prayers during a visit. This can be gained during the octave.

Any day during the octave of the feast of the rosary all the faithful can gain a plenary indulgence. Confession, communion, visit to a chapel of the rosary, and prayers.

Second Sunday: Divine Maternity of the Blessed Virgin Mary.

Archconfraternity of Our Lady of the Sacred Heart. Confession, communion, and prayers during a visit to a confraternity church.

2d. Holy Guardian Angels.

Archconfraternity of the Holy Family (Liège). Confession, communion, visit from first vespers to the confraternity or parish church, and prayers. This indulgence may be gained during the octave.

Blue Scapular of the Immaculate Conception. Confession, communion, visit, and prayers.

Daily recital morning and evening of the prayer "Angel of God," etc. (see page 116). Confession, communion, visit, and prayers.

4th. St. Francis of Assisi.

Promoters of the Apostleship of Prayer. Confession, communion, visit, and prayers.

Third Order of St. Francis. Confession and communion.

9th. St. Denis.

Archconfraternity of the Sacred Heart of Jesus (Montmartre). Confession, communion, and prayers during a visit from first vespers to the parish church.

15th. St. Teresa.

Association of Perpetual Adoration and Work for Poor Churches. Confession, communion, visit to a church of the confraternity, and prayers.

Confraternity of the Scapular of Our Lady of Mount Carmel. Confession, communion, and prayers during a visit to the parish or confraternity church. It may be gained during the octave.

Archconfraternity of St. Joseph (Beauvais). Confession, communion, visit, and prayers.

Blue Scapular of the Immaculate Conception. Confession, communion, visit, and prayers.

Promoters of the Apostleship of Prayer. Confession, communion, visit, and prayers.

17th. Blessed Margaret Mary.

Archconfraternity of the Sacred Heart of Jesus (Montmartre). Confession, communion, and prayers during a visit from first vespers to the parish church.

23d (or in some places the Third Sunday of July). Most Holy Redeemer.

Archconfraternity of the Precious Blood of Jesus Christ. Confession, communion, and visit.

28th. St. Simon and St. Jude, Apostles.

Archconfraternity of St. Joseph (Beauvais). Confession, communion, visit, and prayers.

Bona Mors Society. Confession, communion in a church of the society, and prayers.

Society for the Propagation of the Faith. Confession, communion, and prayers during a visit to the confraternity or parish church.

Apostolic Indulgences. Confession, communion, and prayers.

NOVEMBER.

Month of the Holy Souls in Purgatory.

Those who practise some special devotions every day of the month for the relief of the suffering souls can gain—

1. Seven years and seven quarantines once a day.
2. Plenary indulgence on any day at choice. Confession, communion, and prayers during a visit.

1st. Feast of All Saints.

Association of Perpetual Adoration and Work for Poor Churches. Confession, communion, and prayers during a visit to a church of the association.

Archconfraternity of the Precious Blood. Confession, communion, and visit.

Archconfraternity of the Sacred Heart of Jesus (Rome). Confession, communion, and visit to a confraternity church.

Confraternity of the Holy Rosary. Confession, communion, and visit to a confraternity church.

Society of the Living Rosary. Confession, communion, and prayers during a visit.

Archconfraternity of the Holy Family (Liège). Confession, communion, visit from first vespers to the confraternity or parish church, and prayers. This indulgence may be gained during the octave.

Bona Mors Society. Confession, communion in a church of the association, and prayers.

Blue Scapular of the Immaculate Conception. Confession, communion, visit, and prayers.

Apostolic Indulgences. Confession, communion, and prayers.

"Hail, holy queen," etc., and "We fly to thy patronage," etc. (every day). Confession, communion, and prayers.

198 *Indulgences to be Gained in November.*

2d. *Commemoration of All Souls.*

Association of Perpetual Adoration and Work for Poor Churches. Confession, communion, and prayers during a visit to a church of the association.

Archconfraternity of the Precious Blood of Jesus Christ. Confession, communion, and visit. This indulgence may be gained during the octave.

Archconfraternity of the Sacred Heart of Jesus (Rome). Confession, communion, and visit to a church of the confraternity.

Archconfraternity of the Holy Family (Liège). Confession, communion, visit from first vespers to the confraternity or parish church, and prayers. This indulgence may be gained during the octave.

10*th.* *St. Andrew Avellino.*

Blue Scapular of the Immaculate Conception. Confession, communion, visit, and prayers.

11th. St. Martin.

Promoters of the Apostleship of Prayer. Confession, communion, visit, and prayers.

Archconfraternity of the Sacred Heart of Jesus (Montmartre). Confession, communion, and prayers during a visit from first vespers to the parish church.

13th. St. Stanislaus Kostka.

Association of Perpetual Adoration and Work for Poor Churches. Confession, communion, and prayers during a visit to a confraternity church.

15th. Commemoration of the Deceased Members of the Mount Carmel Order.

Confraternity of the Scapular of Our Lady of Mount Carmel. Confession, communion, and prayers during a visit to the parish or confraternity church.

19th. St. Elizabeth of Hungary.

Third Order of St. Francis. Members can receive the general absolution from first vespers. Confession, communion, and prayers.

Promoters of the Apostleship of Prayer. Confession, communion, visit, and prayers.

21st. *Presentation of the Blessed Virgin.*

Archconfraternity of the Precious Blood of Jesus Christ. Confession, communion, and visit.

Confraternity of the Holy Rosary. (Three indulgences.)

1. Visit to a chapel of the rosary from first vespers.

2. Confession, communion, and prayers during a visit.

3. Procession.

Society of the Living Rosary. Confession, communion, and prayers during a visit.

Confraternity of the Scapular of Our Lady of Mount Carmel. Confession, communion, and prayers during a visit to the parish or confraternity church.

Archconfraternity of the Most Holy and

Immaculate Heart of Mary for the Conversion of Sinners. Confession and communion.

24th. St. John of the Cross.

Confraternity of the Scapular of Our Lady of Mount Carmel. Confession, communion, and prayers during a visit to the confraternity or parish church. This indulgence may be gained during the octave.

30th. St. Andrew, Apostle.

Archconfraternity of St. Joseph (Beauvais). Confession, communion, visit, and prayers.

Bona Mors Society. Confession, communion in a church of the society, and prayers.

Society for the Propagation of the Faith. Confession, communion, and prayers during a visit to the confraternity or parish church.

Apostolic Indulgences. Confession, communion, and prayers.

DECEMBER.

3d. *St. Francis Xavier.*

Association of Perpetual Adoration and Work for Poor Churches. Confession, communion, and prayers during a visit to a church of the society.

Archconfraternity of the Precious Blood of Jesus Christ. Confession, communion, and visit.

Society for the Propagation of the Faith. Confession, communion, and prayers during a visit to the confraternity or parish church. This indulgence may be gained during the octave.

6th. *St. Nicholas.*

Archconfraternity of the Precious Blood of Jesus Christ. Confession, communion, and visit.

8th. *Immaculate Conception of the Blessed Virgin Mary.*

Association of Perpetual Adoration and Work for Poor Churches. Confession, communion, and prayers during a visit to a church of the confraternity.

Archconfraternity of the Precious Blood of Jesus Christ. Confession, communion, and visit. This indulgence may be gained during the octave.

Archconfraternity of the Sacred Heart of Jesus (Rome). Confession, communion, and visit to a church of the confraternity.

Apostleship of Prayer. Confession, communion, and visit, from first vespers, and prayers.

Archconfraternity of Our Lady of the Sacred Heart. Confession, communion, and prayers during a visit, from first vespers, to a church of the confraternity.

Confraternity of the Holy Rosary. (Four indulgences.)

1. Visit to a chapel of the rosary, from first vespers.
2. Confession, communion, and prayers, during a visit.
3. Confession, communion, visit to a chapel of the rosary, and prayers.
4. Procession.

Society of the Living Rosary. Confession, communion, and prayers during a visit.

Confraternity of the Scapular of Our Lady of Mount Carmel. Confession, communion, and prayers during a visit to the confraternity or parish church.

Sodalities of the Blessed Virgin. Confession and communion.

Archconfraternity of the Most Holy and Immaculate Heart of Mary for the Conversion of Sinners. Confession and communion.

Archconfraternity of St. Joseph (Rome and Beauvais). Confession, communion, visit (from first vespers in the Roman confraternity), and prayers.

Archconfraternity of St. Joseph (Angers). Confession, communion, and prayers during a visit to a confraternity church.

Society of the Holy Family. Confession, communion, visit to the parish church, and prayers.

Archconfraternity of the Holy Family (Liège). Confession, communion, visit

from first vespers to the parish or confraternity church, and prayers. This indulgence may be gained during the octave.

Bona Mors Society. Confession, communion in a church of the society, and prayers.

Third Order of St. Francis. Members may receive the general absolution from first vespers. Confession, communion, and prayers.

Blue Scapular of the Immaculate Conception. Confession, communion, visit, and prayers.

Scapular of St. Joseph. Confession, communion, and prayers during a visit from first vespers.

Litany of the Blessed Virgin (every day). Confession, communion, and prayers during a visit.

"Hail, holy queen," etc., and "We fly to thy patronage," etc. (every day). Confession, communion, and prayers.

13th. *St. Lucy.*

Promoters of the Apostleship of Prayer. Confession, communion, visit, and prayers.

Indulgences to be Gained in December.

Blue Scapular of the Immaculate Conception. Confession, communion, visit, and prayers.

16th. *First Day of the Novena for Christmas.*

Blue Scapular of the Immaculate Conception. Confession, communion, visit, and prayers.

21st. *St. Thomas, Apostle.*

Archconfraternity of St. Joseph (Beauvais). Confession, communion, visit, and prayers.

Bona Mors Society. Confession, communion in a church of the society, and prayers.

Society for the Propagation of the Faith. Confession, communion, and prayers during a visit to the confraternity or parish church.

Apostolic Indulgences. Confession, communion, and prayers.

24th. *Last Day of the Novena.*

Indulgence and conditions are the same as on the 16th inst.

25th. Christmas Day.

Archconfraternity of the Precious Blood of Jesus Christ. Confession, communion, and visit. This indulgence may be gained during the octave.

Archconfraternity of Our Lady of the Sacred Heart. Confession, communion, and prayers during a visit from first vespers to the confraternity church.

Confraternity of the Holy Rosary. Confession, communion, and visit to a church of the confraternity.

Society of the Living Rosary. Confession, communion, and prayers during a visit.

Confraternity of the Scapular of Our Lady of Mount Carmel. Confession, communion, and prayers during a visit to the parish or confraternity church.

Sodalities of the Blessed Virgin. Confession and communion.

Archconfraternity of St. Joseph (Rome and Beauvais). Confession, communion, visit (from first vespers in the Roman confraternity), and prayers.

Archconfraternity of St. Joseph (Angers). Confession, communion, and prayers during a visit from first vespers to a church of the confraternity.

Society of the Holy Family. Confession, communion, visit to the parish church, and prayers.

Archconfraternity of the Holy Family (Liège). Confession, communion, visit from first vespers to the parish or confraternity church, and prayers. This indulgence may be gained during the octave.

Bona Mors Society. Confession, communion in a church of the society, and prayers.

Third Order of St. Francis. Members may receive the general absolution from first vespers. Confession, communion, and prayers.

Blue Scapular of the Immaculate Conception. Confession, communion, visit, and prayers.

Scapular of St. Joseph. Confession, communion, and prayers during a visit from first vespers.

Apostolic Indulgences. Confession, communion, and prayers.

Attendance at the explanation of the Gospel (every Sunday). Confession and communion.

Stations of Rome. Confession, communion, visit, and prayers.

Novena as a preparation for Christmas. To all who practise this devotion a plenary indulgence is granted on Christmas day. Confession, communion, and prayers.

Sunday within the Octave of Christmas.

Confraternity of the Holy Rosary. Confession, communion, visit to an altar of the rosary, and prayers.

27th. St. John the Evangelist.

Promoters of the Apostleship of Prayer. Confession, communion, visit, and prayers.

Association of Perpetual Adoration and Work for Poor Churches. Confession, communion, and prayers during a visit to a church of the confraternity.

Archconfraternity of the Sacred Heart

of Jesus (Rome). Confession, communion, and visit to a church of the confraternity.

Archconfraternity of the Most Holy and Immaculate Heart of Mary for the Conversion of Sinners. Confession, communion, and prayers.

Archconfraternity of St. Joseph (Beauvais). Confession, communion, visit, and prayers.

Bona Mors Society. Confession, communion in a church of the society, and prayers.

Society for the Propagation of the Faith. Confession, communion, and prayers during a visit to the parish or confraternity church.

Apostolic Indulgences. Confession, communion, and prayers.

B. Movable Feasts to which are Attached Plenary Indulgences.

I. FEASTS AND DEVOTIONS PRECEDING LENT.

Exposition of the Blessed Sacrament during the Carnival Time.

(For all the Faithful.)

Confession, communion, and prayers during a visit to the Blessed Sacrament while exposed for adoration. This indulgence can be gained only once each year.

Sunday preceding Septuagesima.

Archconfraternity of the Sacred Heart of Jesus (Montmartre). Confession, communion, and prayers during a visit from first vespers to the parish church.

Archconfraternity of the Most Holy and Immaculate Heart of Mary for the Conversion of Sinners. Confession and communion.

Tuesday preceding Septuagesima.

(Prayer of Our Lord in the Garden.)

Apostleship of Prayer—Members of Second Degree. Confession, communion, and prayers during a visit to the confraternity or parish church.

II. LENT.

Every Friday in Lent

(Except Good Friday).

Archconfraternity of the Sacred Heart of Jesus (Montmartre). Confession, communion, and prayers during a visit to a church of the confraternity. The visit must be made between sunrise and sunset.

Any Two Fridays.

Confraternity of the Holy Rosary. Confession, communion, and prayers during a visit.

Every Saturday.

Blue Scapular of the Immaculate Conception. Confession, communion, visit, and prayers.

The many partial indulgences of the stations of Rome may be gained every day during Lent. The conditions are a visit to the proper church and the usual prayers.

III. PASSION WEEK.

(The Week before Holy Week.)

Passion Sunday

Blue Scapular of the Immaculate Conception. Confession, communion, visit, and prayers.

Friday following Passion Sunday.
(Commemoration of the Seven Sorrows of the Blessed Virgin.)

Archconfraternity of the Precious Blood of Jesus Christ. Confession, communion, and visit.

Confraternity of the Holy Rosary. Confession, communion, and visit to a church of the confraternity.

Society of the Living Rosary. Confession, communion, and prayers during a visit.

214 *Indulgences to be Gained in Holy Week.*

Archconfraternity of the Most Holy and Immaculate Heart of Mary for the Conversion of Sinners. Confession and communion.

Archconfraternity of the Holy Family (Liège). Confession, communion, visit from first vespers to the confraternity or parish church, and prayers. This indulgence may be gained during the octave.

Blue Scapular of the Immaculate Conception. Confession, communion, visit, and prayers.

IV. HOLY WEEK.

Wednesday of Holy Week.

Blue Scapular of the Immaculate Conception. Confession, communion, visit, and prayers.

Holy Thursday.

Confraternity of the Blessed Sacrament. Confession, communion, prayers during a visit, and procession.

Archconfraternity of the Precious Blood

of Jesus Christ. Confession, communion, and visit.

Archconfraternity of the Sacred Heart of Jesus (Montmartre). For those who make their adoration in the daytime. Confession, communion, visit, prayers, and one hour of adoration.

Confraternity of the Scapular of Our Lady of Mount Carmel. Confession, communion, and prayers during a visit to the parish or confraternity church.

Archconfraternity of the Holy Family (Liège). Confession, communion, visit from first vespers to the confraternity or parish church, and prayers.

Blue Scapular of the Immaculate Conception. Confession, communion, visit, and prayers.

Holy Hour. Plenary indulgence for those who spend one hour in meditation or prayer in honor of the institution of the Blessed Sacrament. Confession and communion.

The confession and communion for this indulgence may be made on any day of the following week instead of Holy Thursday.

Visit to the Repository either Thursday or Friday morning. Confession, communion, and prayers during a visit. The confession and communion for this indulgence may be made Easter Sunday.

Stations of Rome. Confession, communion, the prescribed visit to a confraternity church, and prayers.

V. EASTER SEASON.

Easter Sunday.

Archconfraternity of the Precious Blood of Jesus Christ. Confession, communion, and visit. This indulgence may be gained during the octave.

Apostleship of Prayer—Members of the Third Degree can gain a plenary indulgence on this day or any other during the Easter time by offering a communion (but not the one by which they fulfil their own Easter obligation) in reparation for those Catholics who offend God by not complying with their Easter duty. There are no other conditions.

Confraternity of the Holy Rosary. (Two indulgences.)

1. Confession, communion, and prayers during a visit.

2. Confession, communion, and a visit to a church of the confraternity.

Society of the Living Rosary. Confession, communion, and prayers during a visit.

Confraternity of the Scapular of Our Lady of Mount Carmel. Confession, communion, and prayers during a visit to the confraternity or parish church.

Archconfraternity of St. Joseph (Beauvais). Confession, communion, visit, and prayers.

Society of the Holy Family. Confession, communion, visit, and prayers.

Archconfraternity of the Holy Family (Liège). Confession, communion, visit from first vespers to the confraternity or parish church, and prayers. This indulgence may be gained during the octave.

Bona Mors Society. Confession, communion in a confraternity church, and prayers.

Third Order of St. Francis. Members may receive the general absolution from first vespers. Confession, communion, and prayers.

Blue Scapular of the Immaculate Conception. Confession, communion, visit, and prayers.

Scapular of St. Joseph. Confession, communion, and prayers during a visit from first vespers.

Apostolic Indulgences. Confession, communion, and prayers.

Stations of Rome. Confession, communion, visit, and prayers.

Attendance at explanation of the Gospel (every Sunday). Confession and communion.

Third Sunday after Easter: Patronage of St. Joseph.

Apostleship of Prayer—Second Degree. Confession, communion, and prayers during a visit to the parish or confraternity church.

Confraternity of the Scapular of Our Lady of Mount Carmel. Confession, communion, and prayers during a visit to the confraternity or parish church. This indulgence may be gained during the octave.

Archconfraternity of Our Lady of the Sacred Heart. Confession, communion, and prayers during a visit from first vespers to a church of the confraternity.

Archconfraternity of St. Joseph (Rome and Beauvais). Confession, communion, visit (from first vespers in the Roman confraternity), and prayers.

Archconfraternity of St. Joseph (Angers). Confession, communion, and prayers during a visit from first vespers to a confraternity church.

Society of the Holy Family. Confession, communion, visit to the parish church, and prayers.

Archconfraternity of the Holy Family (Liège). Confession, communion, visit from first vespers to the confraternity or parish church, and prayers. This indulgence may be gained during the octave.

Bona Mors Society. Confession, communion, and prayers during a visit from first vespers to a church of the society.

Scapular of St. Joseph. Confession, communion, and prayers during a visit, which may be made from first vespers.

Fourth Sunday after Easter.

Archconfraternity of the Sacred Heart of Jesus (Rome). Confession, communion, and prayers during a visit. This indulgence may be gained on the preceding Friday.

Archconfraternity of the Most Holy and Immaculate Heart of Mary for the Conversion of Sinners (St. Aurelia). Confession and communion.

Fifth Sunday after Easter.

Archconfraternity of the Sacred Heart of Jesus (Rome). Confession, communion, and prayers during a visit.

The Ascension of Our Lord.

Archconfraternity of the Precious Blood of Jesus Christ. Confession, communion, visit.

Archconfraternity of Our Lady of the Sacred Heart. Confession, communion, and prayers during a visit from first vespers to a church of the confraternity.

Confraternity of the Holy Rosary. Confession, communion, and prayers during a visit.

Society of the Living Rosary. Confession, communion, and prayers during a visit.

Confraternity of the Scapular of Our Lady of Mount Carmel. Confession, communion, and prayers during a visit to the confraternity or parish church.

Sodalities of the Blessed Virgin. Confession and communion.

Archconfraternity of St. Joseph (Rome and Beauvais). Confession, communion, visit (from first vespers in the Roman confraternity), and prayers.

Society of the Holy Family. Confession, communion, visit to the parish church, and prayers.

Archconfraternity of the Holy Family (Liège). Confession, communion, visit from first vespers to the confraternity or parish church, and prayers. This indulgence may be gained during the octave.

Bona Mors Society. Confession, communion in a church of the society, and prayers.

Blue Scapular of the Immaculate Conception. Confession, communion, visit, and prayers.

Scapular of St. Joseph. Confession, communion, and prayers during a visit from first vespers.

Apostolic Indulgences. Confession, communion, and prayers.

Stations of Rome. Confession, communion, visit to the confraternity church, and prayers.

Sunday (or Friday) following the Ascension.

Archconfraternity of the Sacred Heart of Jesus (Rome). Confession, communion, and prayers during a visit.

Pentecost.

Archconfraternity of the Precious Blood of Jesus Christ. Confession, communion, and visit.

Archconfraternity of the Sacred Heart of Jesus (Rome). Confession, communion, and prayers during a visit. This indulgence may be gained on the preceding Friday.

Confraternity of the Holy Rosary. (Two indulgences.)

1. Confession, communion, and prayers during a visit.

2. Confession, communion, and a visit to a confraternity church.

Society of the Living Rosary. Confession, communion, prayers during a visit.

Archconfraternity of St. Joseph (Rome).

Confession, communion, visit from first vespers, and prayers.

Bona Mors Society. Confession, communion in a confraternity church, and prayers.

Third Order of St. Francis. Members may receive the general absolution from first vespers. Confession, communion, and prayers.

Blue Scapular of the Immaculate Conception. Confession. communion, visit, and prayers.

Apostolic Indulgences. Confession, communion, and prayers.

Attendance at the explanation of the Gospel (every Sunday). Confession and communion.

Monday after Pentecost.

Archconfraternity of the Holy Family (Liège). Confession, communion, visit from first vespers to the parish or confraternity church, and prayers. This indulgence may be gained during the octave.

VI. AFTER THE EASTER SEASON.

First Sunday after Pentecost: The Holy Trinity.

Archconfraternity of the Sacred Heart of Jesus (Rome). Confession, communion, and prayers during a visit. This indulgence may be gained on the preceding Friday.

Society of the Living Rosary. Confession, communion, and prayers during a visit.

Bona Mors Society. Confession, communion in a confraternity church, and prayers.

Blue Scapular of the Immaculate Conception. Confession, communion, visit, and prayers.

Apostolic Indulgences. Confession, communion, and prayers.

Corpus Christi.

Confraternity of the Blessed Sacrament. Confession, communion, procession, and prayers. This indulgence may be gained during the octave.

Association of Perpetual Adoration and Work for Poor Churches. Confession, communion, and prayers during a visit to a confraternity church. This indulgence may be gained during the octave.

Archconfraternity of the Precious Blood of Jesus Christ. Confession, communion, and visit.

Archconfraternity of the Sacred Heart of Jesus (Montmartre). For those who make their adoration in the daytime. Confession, communion, visit, prayers, and one hour of adoration.

Confraternity of the Holy Rosary. Confession, communion, visit to an altar of the rosary, and prayers.

Society of the Living Rosary. Confession, communion, and prayers during a visit.

Archconfraternity of St. Joseph (Rome and Beauvais). Confession, communion, visit (from first vespers in the Roman confraternity), and prayers.

Archconfraternity of the Holy Family (Liège). (Two indulgences.)

1. Confession, communion, visit from first vespers to the parish or confraternity church, and prayers.

2. On the day of the procession of the Blessed Sacrament. Confession, communion, visit from first vespers to the confraternity or parish church, prayers, and participation in the procession. Both of these indulgences may be gained during the octave of the feast.

Bona Mors Society. Confession, communion in a confraternity church, and prayers.

Apostolic Indulgences. Confession, communion, and prayers.

Holy Hour. Those who spend one hour in prayer or meditation in honor of the institution of the Blessed Sacrament. Confession and communion.

Friday (or Sunday) after Corpus Christi.

Archconfraternity of the Sacred Heart of Jesus (Rome). Confession, communion, and prayers during a visit.

Feast of the Sacred Heart of Jesus.

Archconfraternity of the Sacred Heart of Jesus (Rome). Confession, communion, and visit. This indulgence may be gained on the following Sunday. Members of this confraternity may gain a plenary indulgence on each of the six Fridays or Sundays preceding the feast of the Sacred Heart. These indulgences have been mentioned in their proper places.

For all the Faithful. Confession, communion, and prayers during a visit.

Association of Perpetual Adoration and Work for Poor Churches. Confession, communion, and prayers during a visit to the confraternity church.

Apostleship of Prayer. Confession, communion, and prayers during a visit from first vespers.

Archconfraternity of Our Lady of the Sacred Heart. Confession, communion, and prayers during a visit from first vespers to a church of the confraternity.

Confraternity of the Scapular of Our

Special Occasions. 229

Lady of Mount Carmel. Confession, communion, visit to the parish or confraternity church, and prayers.

Archconfraternity of the Holy Family (Liège). Confession, communion, visit from first vespers to the parish or confraternity church, and prayers. This indulgence may be gained during the octave.

Third Order of St. Francis. Members may receive the general absolution from first vespers. Confession, communion, and prayers.

C. Plenary Indulgences which may be gained on Special Occasions during the Year.

1. *During the Forty Hours' Devotion.*

For all the Faithful. Confession, communion, visit to the Blessed Sacrament during the exposition, and prayers.

Confraternity of the Scapular of Our Lady of Mount Carmel. Confession, communion, and prayers during a visit to the parish or confraternity church in which the devotion is being practised.

Sodalities of the Blessed Virgin. Confession, communion, and prayers during a visit to the Blessed Sacrament while exposed in the sodality chapel.

Blue Scapular of the Immaculate Conception. Confession, communion, visit, and prayers. This indulgence can be gained only once a year.

Members of Religious Orders, during the devotion of Forty Hours ordered by their Superiors. Confession, communion, prayers, and to spend at least two hours (at different times) in the prayers prescribed.

2. *Spiritual Retreat.*

Those who spend some days in retreat in a house or church of the Fathers of the Society of Jesus, or elsewhere, under the direction of a Jesuit priest, may gain a plenary indulgence. Confession, communion, and visit to the church in which the exercises have been made.

Children of Mary for a retreat lasting from five to ten days. No condition, except to follow the exercises, which always include confession and communion.

Blue Scapular of the Immaculate Conception. Confession, communion, visit, and prayers. This indulgence can be gained only once a year.

Members of Religious Orders who make a retreat of ten days and meditate at least two hours, at different times, during each day. Confession and communion.

Third Order of St. Francis (for a retreat of eight consecutive days). Confession and communion.

3. *Local and Personal Feasts.*

Confraternity of the Holy Rosary. Feast of the titular patron of the Church. Confession, communion, visit to an altar of the rosary, and prayers.

Sodalities of the Blessed Virgin.

1. Titular feast of the Sodality. Confession, communion, and prayers during a

visit from first vespers to the sodality church.

2. Secondary feast of the Sodality (or, if there is none, on any day appointed by the spiritual director). Confession, communion, and prayers during a visit to the church of the sodality.

Society of the Holy Family. Patronal feast of each member. Confession, communion, visit to the parish church, and prayers.

Archconfraternity of the Holy Family (Liège).

1. Feast of the yearly patron given to each member. Confession, communion, visit from first vespers to the confraternity or parish church, and prayers.

2. Feast of the patron of each section of the confraternity, for all the members of that section. Same conditions as for the preceding indulgence.

3. Feast of the patron saint of the place where the confraternity is established—for all the people of that locality. Same conditions as for the preceding indulgence.

These three indulgences may be gained during the respective octaves of these feasts.

Members of Religious Orders. Principal feast of the Order: Confession, communion, and prayers.

Frequent Communion. For those who practise this devotion. Principal feast of the city or place. Confession, communion, and prayers.

4. *Other Occasions.*

Association of Perpetual Adoration and Work for Poor Churches.

1. Novena of Expiation, celebrated in any church of the association. For those who assist at the exercises at least five times. Confession, communion, and prayers during a visit to a church of the confraternity.

2. General meeting of the members for the purpose of exhibiting their supplies for poor churches. Confession, communion, and prayers during a visit to a church of the confraternity.

Promoters of the Apostleship of Prayer may gain a plenary indulgence twice a year, when they renew their act of consecration, while wearing openly the cross of their rank, provided it be habitually and visibly worn during the year. No other conditions.

Archconfraternity of the Most Holy and Immaculate Heart of Mary for the Conversion of Sinners. On the anniversary of each member's baptism. Confession and communion, and to recite one Hail Mary every day.

Archconfraternity of St. Joseph (Rome). Day on which the Office is said for deceased members. Confession, communion, visit between sunrise and sunset, and prayers.

Archconfraternity of the Holy Family. (Liège). Day of the procession of the Blessed Sacrament. Confession, communion, visit to a confraternity church, prayers, and to take part in the procession.

Society for the Propagation of the Faith.
1. On the occasion of the solemn ser-

vice for all the deceased members. Confession, communion, and prayers during a visit to the church in which the service is being held.

2. On the occasion of Mass or Office for the deceased members of a diocese or section. Same conditions as in the preceding case.

5. *Days Appointed by Superiors.*

Archconfraternity of the Holy Face.

1. On any day designated in the year by the bishop of the diocese. Confession, communion, and prayers during a visit from first vespers to a church of the confraternity.

2. Any four of the monthly meeting days designated by the bishop. Confession, communion, and prayers during a visit to a church of the confraternity.

Third Order of St. Francis. Twice a year when they receive the papal benediction. Conditions: Prayers for the Holy Father's intentions.

6. Days to be Selected in the Year by the Individual.

Association of Perpetual Adoration and Work for Poor Churches. Any two days in the year on which they receive communion for the deceased members. Confession and prayers during a visit to a church of the confraternity.

Society of the Living Rosary. For those who have recited the daily decade throughout the year. Confession, communion, and prayers.

Blue Scapular of the Immaculate Conception. Confession, communion, visit, and prayers.

Rosary of the Blessed Virgin. Plenary indulgence on any one day in the year for those who say five decades every day. Confession, communion, and prayers.

Act of Conformity to the Will of God (every day). "May the most just," etc. (see page 104). Confession, communion, and prayers.

B. Plenary Indulgences which may be gained in Varying Circumstances of Life.

1. *First Mass of a Priest.*

1. For the priest. Confession, visit, and prayers.
2. For his relatives, to the third degree inclusive, who assist at this Mass. Confession, communion, and prayers.
3. For all members of Religious Orders who assist at the first Mass of a member of a Religious Order. Communion.

2. *Receiving the Religious Habit and Making the Solemn Profession.*

A plenary indulgence is granted on each of these days. Confession and communion.

3. *Reception into a Confraternity or Pious Association.*

Confession, communion, visit, and prayers.

4. *For the Sick.*

A plenary indulgence if they receive holy communion, say three Our Fathers and Hail Marys in the presence of a crucifix, and resolve to accept death with resignation as coming from the hand of God.

5. *In the Hour of Death.*

The plenary indulgence for a happy death is attached (*a*) to almost all scapulars and religious confraternities, (*b*) to objects enriched with the apostolic indulgences, (*c*) to the frequent invocation of the holy name of Jesus during life, (*d*) to the frequent recital during life of the prayer to the guardian angel, of the acts of faith, hope, and charity, and of the act of conformity with the Divine Will.

The conditions usually required for gaining this indulgence are:

1. To receive the last sacraments, if possible.

2. To invoke orally, or at least mentally, the holy name of Jesus.

3. To accept death with resignation, as sent by God.

A person may be entitled to this indulgence on many grounds, but it can be received only once, and that time is the very moment of death, not at the time the conditions are complied with.

This indulgence is not applicable to the souls in purgatory.

All that is necessary to gain it is to comply with the conditions prescribed by the Church.

All the faithful, at the point of death, may receive the apostolic blessing and plenary indulgence from a priest who has the necessary faculties for granting same.

Standard Catholic Books

PUBLISHED BY

BENZIGER BROTHERS,

CINCINNATI: NEW YORK: CHICAGO:
343 MAIN ST. 36 & 38 BARCLAY ST. 178 MONROE ST.

ABANDONMENT; or, Absolute Surrender to Divine Providence. 32mo, *net*, 0 40
ANALYSIS OF THE GOSPELS for the Sundays and Holydays. Lambert. 12mo, *net*, 1 25
ART OF PROFITING BY OUR FAULTS. 32mo, *net*, 0 40
BIBLE, THE HOLY. 12mo, cloth, 1 25
BIRTHDAY SOUVENIR, OR DIARY. 32mo, 0 50
BLESSED ONES OF 1888. 16mo, illustrated, 0 50
BLIND FRIEND OF THE POOR: Reminiscences of the Life and Works of Mgr. de Ségur. 16mo, 0 50
BLISSYLVANIA POST-OFFICE, THE. By M. A. Taggart. 16mo, 0 50
BOYS' AND GIRLS' ANNUAL. 0 05
BOYS' AND GIRLS' MISSION BOOK. By the Redemptorists. 48mo, 0 35
BROWNSON, ORESTES A., Literary, Scientific, and Political Views of. 12mo, *net*, 1 25
BUGG, LELIA HARDIN. The Correct Thing for Catholics. 16mo, 0 75
—— A Lady. Manners and Social Usages. 16mo, 1 00
CANTATA CATHOLICA. A collection of Masses, etc. 4to, *net*, 2 00
CATECHISM OF FAMILIAR THINGS. 12mo, 1 00
CATHOLIC BELIEF. 16mo,
   Paper, 0.25; 25 copies, 4.25; 50 copies, 7.50; 100 copies, 12.50
   Cloth, 0.50; 25 copies, 8.50; 50 copies, 15.00; 100 copies, 25.00

CATHOLIC FAMILY LIBRARY. Composed of "The Christian Father," "The Christian Mother," "Sure Way to a Happy Marriage," "Instructions on the Commandments and Sacraments," and "Stories for First Communicants." 5 volumes in box. 2 00

CATHOLIC HOME ANNUAL. 0 25

CATHOLIC HOME LIBRARY. 10 vols. 12mo, each, 0 45

CATHOLIC CEREMONIES and Explanation of the Ecclesiastical Year. By the Abbé Durand. 24mo. Paper, 0.25; 25 copies, 4.25; 50 copies, 7.50; 100 copies, 12 50
Cloth, 0.50; 25 copies, 8.50; 50 copies, 15.00; 100 copies, 25 00
Contains an explanation of the ceremonies and prayers at Mass, a paraphrase of the Vesper psalms, short and clear instructions on the principal feasts and the different seasons of the ecclesiastical year.

CATHOLIC WORSHIP. The Sacraments, Ceremonies, and Festivals of the Church Explained.
Paper, 0.15; per 100, 9.00. Cloth, 0.25; per 100, 15 00

CATHOLIC YOUNG MAN OF THE PRESENT DAY. Egger. 32mo, 0.25; per 100, 15 00

CHARITY THE ORIGIN OF EVERY BLESSING. 16mo, 0 75

CHILD OF MARY. A complete Prayer-Book for Children of Mary. 32mo, 0 60

CHRIST IN TYPE AND PROPHECY. Maas. 2 vols., 12mo, *net*, 4 00

CHRISTIAN ANTHROPOLOGY. Thein. 8vo. *net*, 2 50

CHRISTIAN FATHER, THE. Paper, 0.25; per 100, 12.50. Cloth, 0.35; per 100, 21 00

CHRISTIAN MOTHER, THE. Paper, 0.25; per 100, 12.50. Cloth, 0.35; per 100, 21 00

CIRCUS-RIDER'S DAUGHTER, THE. A novel. By F. v. Brackel. 12mo, 1 25

CLARKE, REV. RICHARD F., S.J. The Devout Year. Short Meditations. 24mo, *net*, 0 60

—— Maria Magnificata. Short Meditations for May. 24mo, flex., 0.15; per 100, 10 00

COCHEM'S EXPLANATION OF THE MASS. See under *Explanation*.

COCHEM'S LIFE OF CHRIST. See under *Life*.

COMEDY OF ENGLISH PROTESTANTISM, THE. Edited
by A. F. Marshall. 12mo, *net*, 0 50
COMPENDIUM SACRÆ LITURGIÆ, Juxta Ritum
Romanum. Wapelhorst. 8vo, *net*, 2 50
CONNOR D'ARCY'S STRUGGLES. A novel. By Mrs.
W. M. Bertholds. 12mo, 1 25
COUNSELS OF A CATHOLIC MOTHER to Her
Daughter. 16mo, 0 50
CROWN OF MARY, THE. A Manual of Devotion for
Clients of the Blessed Virgin. 32mo, 0 60
CROWN OF THORNS, THE. 32mo, 0 50
DATA OF MODERN ETHICS EXAMINED, THE. Ming.
12mo, *net*, 2 00
DAY OF FIRST COMMUNION. Paper, 5 cents; per
100, 3 00
DE GOESBRIAND, RIGHT REV. L. Christ on the
Altar. 4to, cloth, richly illustrated, gilt edges, 6 00
——— Jesus the Good Shepherd. 16mo, *net*, 0 75
——— The Labors of the Apostles. 12mo, *net*, 1 00
DEVOTIONS AND PRAYERS BY ST. ALPHONSUS. A
complete Prayer-Book. 16mo, 1 00
EGAN, MAURICE F. The Vocation of Edward
Conway. A novel. 12mo, 1 25
——— The Flower of the Flock, 12mo, 1 00
——— How They Worked Their Way. 12mo, 1 00
——— A Gentleman. 16mo, 0 75
——— The Boys in the Block. 24mo, leatherette, 0 25
ENGLISH READER. Edited by Rev. Edward Connolly, S. J. 12mo, 1 25
EPISTLES AND GOSPELS. 32mo, 0 25
EUCHARISTIC CHRIST, THE. By Rev. A. Tesnière.
12mo, *net*, 1 00
EUCHARISTIC GEMS. 16mo, 0 75
EVE OF THE REFORMATION. By Rev. Wm. Stang,
D.D. 12mo, paper, *net*, 0 50
EXAMINATION OF CONSCIENCE for the use of
Priests. 32mo, *net*, 0 30
EXPLANATION OF THE BALTIMORE CATECHISM.
Kinkead. 12mo, *net*, 1 00
EXPLANATION OF THE COMMANDMENTS, ILLUSTRATED. By Rev. H. Rolfus, D.D. 16mo, 0 75
An explanation of the Commandments of God and
of the Church, with numerous examples, etc.

EXPLANATION OF THE GOSPELS and Explanation of Catholic Worship. 24mo, illustrated.
Paper, 0.25; 25 copies, 4.25; 50 copies, 7.50; 100 copies, 12 50
Cloth, 0.50; 25 copies, 8.50; 50 copies, 15.00; 100 copies, 25 00
EXPLANATION OF THE OUR FATHER AND THE HAIL MARY. Brennan. 16mo, 0 75
EXPLANATION OF THE MASS. By Father M. von Cochem. 12mo, 1 25
EXPLANATION OF THE PRAYERS AND CEREMONIES OF THE MASS, ILLUSTRATED. By Rev. I. D. Lanslots, O.S.B. With 22 full-page pictures. 12mo, 1 25
EXPLANATION OF THE SALVE REGINA. Liguori. 16mo, 0 75
EXTREME UNCTION. Paper, 10 cents; per 100, 5 00
The same in German at the same prices.
FABIOLA; or, The Church of the Catacombs. By Cardinal Wiseman. Illus. Edition. 12mo, 1 25
Edition de luxe, 6 00
FATAL DIAMONDS, THE. By E. C. Donnelly. 24mo, leatherette, 0 25
FINN, REV. FRANCIS, J., S.J. Percy Wynn; or, Making a Boy of Him. 12mo, 0 85
—— Tom Playfair; or, Making a Start. 12mo, 0 85
—— Harry Dee; or, Working it Out. 12mo, 0 85
—— Claude Lightfoot; or, How the Problem was Solved. 12mo, 0 85
—— Mostly Boys. 12mo, 0 85
—— Ethelred Preston; or, The Adventures of a Newcomer. 12mo, 0 85
—— That Football Game: and What Came of It. 12mo, 0 85
—— My Strange Friend. 24mo, leatherette. 0 25
FIRST COMMUNICANT'S MANUAL. Small 32mo, 0 50
FIVE O'CLOCK STORIES. 16mo, 0 75
FLOWERS OF THE PASSION. 32mo 0 50
FOLLOWING OF CHRIST, THE. By Thomas à Kempis. With Reflections. Small 32mo, cloth, 0 50
Without Reflections. Small 32mo, cloth, 0 45
Edition de luxe. Illustrated, from 1 50 up.
FRANCIS DE SALES, ST. Guide for Confession and Communion. 32mo, 0 60

FRANCIS DE SALES, ST. Maxims and Counsels for Every Day. 32mo, 0 50
—— New Year Greetings. 32mo, flexible cloth, 15 cents; per 100, 10 00
GENERAL PRINCIPLES OF THE RELIGIOUS LIFE. Verheyen. 32mo, *net*, 0 30
GLORIES OF DIVINE GRACE. Scheeben. 12mo, *net*, 1 50
GLORIES OF MARY, THE. Liguori. 2 vols. 12mo, *net*, 2 50
GOD KNOWABLE AND KNOWN. Ronayne, S.J. 12mo, *net*, 1 25
GOFFINE'S DEVOUT INSTRUCTIONS. Illustrated edition. With Preface by His Eminence Cardinal Gibbons. 8vo, cloth, 1.00; 10 copies, 7.50; 25 copies, 17.50; 50 copies, 33 50

This is the best, the cheapest, and the most popular illustrated edition of Goffine's Instructions.

"GOLDEN SANDS," Books by the Author of Golden Sands, Little Counsels for the Sanctification and Happiness of Daily Life. Third, Fourth, Fifth Series. 32mo. each, 0 60
Also in finer bindings.
—— Book of the Professed. 32mo.
  Vol. I. ⎫   ⎧ *net*, 0 75
  Vol. II. ⎬ Each with a Steel-Plate   ⎨ *net*, 0 60
  Vol. III.⎭   Frontispiece.   ⎩ *net*, 0 60
—— Prayer. 32mo, *net*, 0 40
—— The Little Book of Superiors. 32mo, *net*, 0 60
—— Spiritual Direction. 32mo, *net*, 0 60
—— Little Month of May. 32mo, flexible cloth, 0 25
—— Little Month of the Souls in Purgatory. 32mo, flexible, 0 25
—— Hints on Letter-Writing. 16mo, 0 60
GROU, REV. N., S.J. The Characteristics of True Devotion. 16mo, *net*, 0 75
——. The Interior of Jesus and Mary. 16mo, 2 vols., *net*, 2 00
HANDBOOK FOR ALTAR SOCIETIES, and Guide for Sacristans. 16mo, *net*, 0 75
HANDBOOK OF THE CHRISTIAN RELIGION. By Rev. W. Wilmers, S.J. 12mo, *net*, 1 50
HAPPY YEAR, A. Lasausse. 12mo, *net*, 1 00
HEART, THE, OF ST. JANE FRANCES DE CHANTAL. Thoughts and Prayers. 32mo, *net*, 0 40
HEIR OF DREAMS, AN. O'Malley. 16mo, 0 50

HELP FOR THE POOR SOULS IN PURGATORY. Small 32mo, 0 50
HIDDEN TREASURE; or, The Value and Excellence of the Holy Mass. 32mo, 0 50
HISTORY OF THE CATHOLIC CHURCH. By Dr. H. Brueck. 2 vols., 8vo, *net*, 3 00
HISTORY OF THE CATHOLIC CHURCH. Brennan-Shea. Illus. 8vo, 1 50
HISTORY OF THE MASS and its Ceremonies. O'Brien. 12mo, *net*, 1 25
HOLY FACE OF JESUS, THE. 32mo, 0 50
HOURS BEFORE THE ALTAR. De La Bouillerie. 32mo, 0 50
HOW TO GET ON. Feeney. 12mo, cloth, 1 00
HOW TO MAKE THE MISSION. 16mo, paper, 0.10; per 100, 5 00
HUNOLT'S SERMONS. Translated by the Rev. J. Allen, D.D. 12 vols., *net*, 30 00
Per set of 2 vols., *net*, 5 00
    Vols. 1, 2. The Christian State of Life.
    Vols. 3, 4. The Bad Christian.
    Vols. 5, 6. The Penitent Christian.
    Vols. 7, 8. The Good Christian.
    Vols. 9, 10. The Christian's Last End.
    Vols. 11, 12. The Christian's Model.

His Eminence Cardinal Satolli, Pro-Delegate Apostolic: ". . . I believe that in it is found realized desire of the Holy Father, who not long ago in an encyclical urged so strongly the return to the simple, unaffected, but earnest and eloquent preaching of the word of God. . . ."

IDOLS; or, The Secret of the Rue Chaussée d'Antin. A novel. By Raoul de Navery. 12mo, 1 25
ILLUSTRATED PRAYER-BOOK FOR CHILDREN. 32mo, 0 25
IMITATION OF THE BLESSED VIRGIN MARY. Small 32mo, 0 50
  Edition de luxe. Printed on India paper, and containing fine half-tone illustrations. 1 50
INSTRUCTIONS ON THE COMMANDMENTS and the Sacraments. By St. Liguori. 32mo, paper, 0.25; per 100, 12.50; cloth, 0.35; per 100, 21 00
KONINGS THEOLOGIA MORALIS. Novissimi Ecclesiæ Doctoris S. Alphonsi. 2 vols. in one, half mor., *net*, 4 00

KONINGS, Commentarium in Facultates Apostolicas. New, greatly enlarged edition. 12mo,
net, 2 25
—— General Confession Made Easy. 32mo, flexible, 0 15
The same in German at the same prices.
LEGENDS AND STORIES OF THE HOLY CHILD JESUS from Many Lands. 16mo, 0 75
LEPER QUEEN, THE. A Story of the Thirteenth Century. 16mo, 0 50
LETTERS OF ST. ALPHONSUS LIGUORI. 5 vols. 12mo, each, *net*, 1 25
LIFE AND ACTS OF LEO XIII. Illustrated. 8vo, 2 00
LIFE OF ST. ALOYSIUS GONZAGA. Cepari-Goldie. Edition de luxe. 8vo, *net*, 2 50
LIFE OF CHRIST. Illustrated. Cochem. With fine half-tone illustrations. 12mo, 1 25
LIFE OF THE BLESSED VIRGIN. Illustrated. Adapted by Rev. Richard Brennan, LL.D. With fine half-tone illustrations. 12mo, 1 25
LIFE OF FATHER CHARLES SIRE. 12mo, *net*, 1 00
LIFE OF ST. CLARE OF MONTEFALCO. 12mo, *net*, 0 75
LIFE OF THE VEN. CRESCENTIA HÖSS. 12mo, *net*, 1 25
LIFE OF MOTHER FONTBONNE. 12mo, *net*, 1 25
LIFE OF ST. FRANCIS SOLANUS. 16mo, *net*, 0 50
LIFE OF ST. GERMAINE COUSIN. 16mo, 0 50
LIFE OF ST. CHANTAL. *net*, 4 00
(LIFE OF) MOST REV. JOHN HUGHES. Brann. 12mo, *net*, 0 75
LIFE OF FATHER JOGUES. 12mo, *net*, 0 75
LIFE OF MLLE. LE GRAS. 12mo, *net*, 1 25
LIFE OF MARY FOR CHILDREN. 24mo, ill., *net*, 0 50
LIFE OF BISHOP NEUMANN. 12mo, *net*, 1 25
LIFE OF FATHER FRANCIS POILVACHE. 32mo, paper, *net*, 0 20
LIFE, POPULAR, OF ST. TERESA. 12mo, *net*, 0 75
LIFE OF OUR LORD AND SAVIOUR JESUS CHRIST.
No. 1. Roan back, gold title, plain cloth sides, sprinkled edges, *net*, 5 00
Also in finer bindings.

LIGUORI, ST. ALPHONSUS DE, Complete Ascetical Works of. Centenary Edition. Per vol. *net*, 1 25

Preparation for Death.
Way of Salvation and of Perfection.
Great Means of Salvation and Perfection.
Incarnation, Birth, and Infancy of Christ.
The Passion and Death of Christ.
The Holy Eucharist.
The Glories of Mary, 2 vols.
Victories of the Martyrs.

True Spouse of Christ, 2 vols.
Dignity and Duties of the Priest.
The Holy Mass.
The Divine Office.
Preaching.
Abridged Sermons for all the Sundays.
Miscellany.
Letters, 4 vols.
Letters and General Index.

LINKED LIVES. A novel. By Lady Douglas. 8vo, 1 50
LITTLE MANUAL OF ST. ANTHONY. Illustrated. 32mo, cloth, 0 60
LITTLE CHILD OF MARY. Large 48mo, 0 35
LITTLE PICTORIAL LIVES OF THE SAINTS. With nearly 400 illustrations. 12mo, 1 00
   10 copies, 6.25; 25 copies, 15.00; 50 copies, 27.50; 100 copies, 50 00
Has the approbation of 39 Archbishops and Bishops.
LITTLE PRAYER-BOOK OF THE SACRED HEART. Sm. 32mo, cloth, 0 40
Also in finer bindings.
LITTLE OFFICE OF THE IMMACULATE CONCEPTION. 32mo, paper, 3 cents; per 100, 1 50
LITTLE SAINT OF NINE YEARS. 16mo, 0 50
LOURDES. Clarke. 16mo. Illustrated, 0 75
LUTHER'S OWN STATEMENTS. O'Connor. 12mo, paper, 0 15
MANIFESTATION OF CONSCIENCE. Confessions and Communions in Religious Communities. 32mo, *net*, 0 50
MCCALLEN, REV. JAMES A., S.S. Sanctuary Boy's Illustrated Manual. 12mo, *net*, 0 50
—— Office of Tenebræ. 12mo, *net*, 1 00
—— Appendix. Containing Harmonizations of the Lamentations. 12mo, *net*, 0 75

MANUAL OF THE HOLY EUCHARIST. Conferences and Pious Practices, with Devotions for Mass, etc. By Rev. F. X. Lasance. Oblong 24mo. 0 75

MANUAL OF THE HOLY FAMILY. 32mo, cloth, 0 60
Also in finer bindings.

MANUAL OF INDULGENCED PRAYERS. Small 32mo, cloth, 0 40
Also in finer bindings.

MARCELLA GRACE. A novel. By Rosa Mulholland. Illustrated. 12mo, 1 25

MARRIAGE. Monsabré, O.P. 12mo, *net*, 1 00

MEANS OF GRACE, THE. A Complete Exposition of the Seven Sacraments, of the Sacramentals, and of Prayer, with a Comprehensive Explanation of the "Lord's Prayer" and the "Hail Mary." By Rev. Richard Brennan, LL.D. With 180 full-page and other illustrations. 8vo, cloth, 2.50; gilt edges, 3.00; Library edition, half levant, 3 50

MEDITATIONS (CHAIGNON), FOR THE USE OF THE SECULAR CLERGY. From the French, by Rt. Rev. L. de Goesbriand, D.D. 2 vols., 8vo, *net*, 4 00

MEDITATIONS (BAXTER) for Every Day in the Year. By Rev. Roger Baxter, S.J. Small 12mo, *net*, 1 25

MEDITATIONS (HAMON'S) FOR ALL THE DAYS OF THE YEAR. For the use of Priests, Religious, and the Laity. By Rev. M. Hamon, S.S. From the French, by Mrs. Anne R. Bennett-Gladstone. 5 vols., 16mo, *net*, 5 00

"Hamon's doctrine is the unadulterated word of God, presented with unction, exquisite taste, and freed from that exaggerated and sickly sentimentalism which disgusts when it does not mislead." —Most Rev. P. L. Chapelle, D.D.

MEDITATIONS (PERINALDO) on the Sufferings of Jesus Christ. 12mo, *net*, 0 75

MEDITATIONS (VERCRUYSSE) for Every Day in the Year. 2 vols., *net*, 2 75

MEDITATIONS ON THE PASSION OF OUR LORD. 32mo, 0 40

MISSION BOOK OF THE REDEMPTORIST FATHERS. 32mo, 0 50

MISSION BOOK FOR THE MARRIED. By Very Rev. F. Girardey, C.SS.R. 32mo, 0 50

MISSION BOOK FOR THE SINGLE. By Very Rev. F. Girardey, C.SS.R. 32mo, 0 50
MISTRESS OF NOVICES, THE, Instructed in her Duties. Leguay. 12mo, cloth, *net*, 0 75
MOMENTS BEFORE THE TABERNACLE. Russell. 24mo, *net*, 0 40
MONK'S PARDON. Raoul de Navery. 12mo, 1 25
MONTH OF THE DEAD. 32mo, 0 75
MONTH OF MAY. Debussi. 32mo, 0 50
MONTH OF THE SACRED HEART. Huguet. 32mo, 0 75
MONTH, NEW, OF MARY, St. Francis de Sales. 32mo, 0 40
MONTH, NEW, OF THE SACRED HEART, St. Francis de Sales. 32mo, 0 40
MONTH, NEW, OF ST. JOSEPH, St. Francis de Sales. 32mo, 0 40
MONTH, NEW, OF THE HOLY ANGELS, St. Francis de Sales. 32mo, 0 40
MOOTED QUESTIONS OF HISTORY. By H. Desmond. 16mo, 0 75
MR. BILLY BUTTONS. By Walter Lecky. 12mo, 1 25
MULLER. REV. MICHAEL, C.SS.R. God the Teacher of Mankind. 9 vols., 8vo. Per set, *net*, 9 50
    The Church and Her Enemies. *net*, 1 10
    The Apostles' Creed. *net*, 1 10
    The First and Greatest Commandment. *net*, 1 40
    Explanation of the Commandments, continued. Precepts of the Church. *net*, 1 10
    Dignity, Authority, and Duties of Parents, Ecclesiastical and Civil Powers. Their Enemies. *net*, 1 40
    Grace and the Sacraments. *net*, 1 25
    Holy Mass. *net*, 1 25
    Eucharist and Penance. *net*, 1 10
    Sacramentals—Prayer, etc. *net*, 1 00
    Familiar Explanation of Catholic Doctrine. 12mo, 1 00
—— The Prodigal Son. 8vo, *net*, 1 00
—— The Devotion of the Holy Rosary. 8vo, *net*, 0 75
—— The Catholic Priesthood. 2 vols., 8vo, *net*, 3 00

MY FIRST COMMUNION : The Happiest Day of My
Life. 16mo, illustrated, 0 75
NAMES THAT LIVE IN CATHOLIC HEARTS. By Anna
T. Sadlier, 12mo, 1 00
NEW RULE OF THE THIRD ORDER OF ST. FRANCIS.
32mo, 5 cents; per 100, 3 00
NEW TESTAMENT, THE. Illus. edition. With 100
full-page illustrations. In two colors. 16mo,
net, 0 60
OFFICE, COMPLETE, OF HOLY WEEK. Latin and
English. 24mo, cloth, 0.50; cloth, limp, gilt
edges, 1 00
Also in finer bindings.
O'GRADY, ELEANOR. Aids to Correct and Effective
Elocution. 12mo, 1 25
—— Select Recitations for Schools and Academies.
12mo, 1 00
—— Readings and Recitations for Juniors.
16mo, *net*, 0 50
—— Elocution Class. A Simplification of the
Laws and Principles of Expression. 16mo, *net*, 0 50
ON CHRISTIAN ART. By Edith Healy. 16mo, 0 50
ON THE ROAD TO ROME, and How Two Brothers
Got There. By William Richards. 16mo, 0 50
ONE AND THIRTY DAYS WITH BLESSED MARGARET
MARY. 32mo, flexible cloth, 0 25
ONE ANGEL MORE IN HEAVEN. White mar., 0 50
OUR BIRTHDAY BOUQUET. Donnelly. 16mo, 1 00
OUR LADY OF GOOD COUNSEL IN GENAZZANO. By
Anne R. Bennett, née Gladstone. 32mo, 0 75
OUR FAVORITE DEVOTIONS. By Very Rev. Dean
A. A. Lings. 24mo, 0 60
Contains all devotions in one volume.
OUR FAVORITE NOVENAS. By Very Rev. Dean
A. A. Lings. 24mo, 0 60
Contains in one volume forms of novenas for the
feasts of Our Lord, the Blessed Virgin, and the
Saints.
OUR YOUNG FOLKS' LIBRARY. 10 volumes. 12mo,
each, 0 45
OUTLAW OF CAMARGUE, THE. De Lamothe. 12mo,
1 25

OUTLINES OF DOGMATIC THEOLOGY. By Rev.
Sylvester J. Hunter, S.J. 3 vols., 12mo, *net*, 4 50
PARADISE ON EARTH OPENED TO ALL.
32mo, *net*, 0 40
PASSING SHADOWS. By Anthony Yorke. 12mo, 1 25
PEARLS FROM FABER. Selected and arranged by
Marion J. Brunowe. 32mo, 0 50
PETRONILLA, and other Stories. Donnelly.
12mo, 1 00
PEW-RENT RECEIPT BOOK. 800 receipts. *net*, 1 00
PHILOSOPHY, ENGLISH MANUALS OF CATHOLIC.
Logic. 12mo. *net*, 1 25
First Principles of Knowledge. 12mo, *net*, 1 25
Moral Philosophy (Ethics and Natural Law).
12mo, *net*, 1 25
Natural Theology. 12mo, *net*, 1 50
Psychology. 12mo. *net*, 1 50
General Metaphysics. 12mo, *net*, 1 25
A Manual of Political Economy. 12mo, *net*, 1 50
PICTORIAL LIVES OF THE SAINTS. With Reflections. 8vo, 2 00
5 copies, 6.65; 10 copies, 12.50; 25 copies, 27.50; 50 copies, 50 00
POPULAR INSTRUCTIONS ON MARRIAGE. By Very
Rev. F. Girardey, C.SS.R. 32mo. Paper, 0.25;
per 100, 12.50; cloth, 0.35; per 100, 21 00
POPULAR INSTRUCTIONS TO PARENTS on the Bringing Up of Children. By Very Rev. F. Girardey,
C.SS.R. 32mo. Paper, 0.25; per 100, 12.50; cloth,
0.35; per 100, 21 00
PRAYER. The Great Means of Obtaining Salvation.
Liguori. 32mo, cloth, 0 50
PRAYER-BOOK FOR LENT. 32mo, cloth, 0 50
PRAXIS SYNODALIS. Manuale Synodi Diocesanæ
ac Provincialis Celebrande. 12mo, *net*, 0 60
PRIEST IN THE PULPIT, THE. A Manual of Homiletics and Catechetics. 8vo, *net*, 1 50
PRIMER FOR CONVERTS, A. Durward. 32mo, flexible cloth, 0 25
PRINCIPLES OF ANTHROPOLOGY AND BIOLOGY.
Hughes. 16mo, *net*, 0 75
READING AND THE MIND, WITH SOMETHING TO
READ. O'Conor, S.J. 12mo, *net*, 1 00

REASONABLENESS OF CATHOLIC CEREMONIES AND PRACTICES. Burke. 32mo, flexible cloth, 0 35
RELIGIOUS STATE, THE. Liguori. 32mo, 0 50
REMINISCENCES OF RT. REV. EDGAR P. WADHAMS, D.D. Walworth. 12mo, illustrated, *net*, 1 00
RIGHTS OF OUR LITTLE ONES; or, First Principles on Education, in Catechetical Form. Conway. 32mo, paper, 0.15; per 100, 9.00. Cloth, 0.25; per 100, 15 00
ROSARY, THE MOST HOLY, in Thirty-one Meditations, Prayers and Examples. Grimm. 32mo, 0 50
ROUND TABLE, A, of the Representative American Catholic Novelists. Containing the best stories by the best writers. With fine half-tone portraits printed in colors, biographical sketches, etc. 12mo, 1 50
RUSSO, N., S.J. DePhilosophia Morali Prælectiones in Collegio Georgiopolitano Soc. Jes. Anno 1889-90 Habitæ. 8vo, half leather, *net*, 2 00
ST. CHANTAL AND THE FOUNDATION OF THE VISITATION. Bougaud. 2 vols., 8vo, *net*, 4 00
ST. JOSEPH, THE ADVOCATE OF HOPELESS CASES. Huguet. 24mo, 1 00
SACRAMENTALS OF THE HOLY CATHOLIC CHURCH, THE. By Rev. A. A. Lambing, LL.D. illus. 24mo. Paper, 0.25; 25 copies, 4.25; 50 copies, 7.50; 100 copies, 12 50
Cloth, 0.50; 25 copies, 8.50; 50 copies, 15.00; 100 copies. 25 00
SACRED HEART, BOOKS ON THE.
Child's Prayer-Book of the Sacred Heart. Small 32mo, 0 20
Devotions for the First Friday. Huguet. 32mo, 0 40
Little Prayer-Book of the Sacred Heart. Small 32mo, 0 40
Imitation of the Sacred Heart. Arnoudt. 16mo, 1 25
Month of the Sacred Heart. Huguet. 32mo, 0 75
New Month of the Sacred Heart. 32mo, 0 40
One and Thirty Days with Blessed Margaret Mary. 32mo, flexible 0 25
Pearls from the Casket of the Sacred Heart. 32mo, 0 50
Month of the Sacred Heart for the Young Christian. By Brother Phillippe. 32mo, 0 50

SACRED HEART, BOOKS ON THE—Continued.
Sacred Heart Studied in the Sacred Scriptures.
Saintrain. 8vo, *net*, 2 00
Revelations of the Sacred Heart to Blessed Margaret Mary. Bougaud. 8vo, *net*, 1 50
Six Sermons on Devotion to the Sacred Heart.
16mo, *net*, 0 60
Year of the Sacred Heart. 32mo, 0 50
SACRED RHETORIC. 12mo, *net*, 0 75
SACRIFICE OF THE MASS. Worthily Celebrated. By Rev. Father Chaignon, S.J. Translated by Right Rev. L. de Goesbriand. 8vo, 1 50
SECRET OF SANCTITY, THE. 12mo, *net*, 1 00
SERAPHIC GUIDE. Manual for the Third Order, 0 60
Roan, red edges, 0 75
SERMONS ON THE BLESSED VIRGIN. McDermott.
16mo, *net*, 0 75
SERMONS for the Sundays and Chief Festivals of the Ecclesiastical Year. By Rev. Julius Pottgeisser, S.J. 2 vols., 8vo, *net*, 2 50
SERMONS, SHORT, FOR LOW MASSES. Schouppe.
12mo, *net*, 1 25
SERMONS, SIX, on Devotion to the Sacred Heart of Jesus. Bierbaum. 16mo, *net*, 0 60
SERMONS ON THE CHRISTIAN VIRTUES. By the Rev. F. Hunolt, S.J. Translated by Rev. J. Allen, D.D. 2 vols., 8vo, *net*, 5 00
SERMONS ON THE DIFFERENT STATES OF LIFE. By Rev. F. Hunolt, S.J. Translated by Rev. J. Allen, D.D. 2 vols., 8vo, *net*, 5 00
SERMONS ON THE SEVEN DEADLY SINS. By Rev. F. Hunolt, S.J. Translated by Rev. J. Allen, D.D. 2 vols., 8vo, *net*, 5 00
SERMONS ON PENANCE. By Rev. F. Hunolt S.J. Translated by Rev. J. Allen, D.D. 2 vols., 8vo, *net*, 5 00
SERMONS ON OUR LORD, THE BLESSED VIRGIN, AND THE SAINTS. By Rev. F. Hunolt, S.J. Translated by Rev. J. Allen, D.D. 2 vols., 8vo, *net*, 5 00
SERMONS, Abridged, for all the Sundays and Holydays. Liguori. 12mo, *net*, 1 25
SERMONS ON THE MOST HOLY ROSARY. By Rev. M. J. Fringa. 12mo, *net*, 1 00

SHORT CONFERENCES ON THE LITTLE OFFICE.
Rainer. 32mo, 0 50
SHORT STORIES ON CHRISTIAN DOCTRINE. 12mo,
illustrated, *net*, 0 75
SMITH, Rev. S. B., D.D. Elements of Ecclesiastical
Law.
Vol. I. Ecclesiastical Persons. 8vo, *net*, 2 50
Vol. II. Ecclesiastical Trials. 8vo, *net*, 2 50
Vol. III. Ecclesiastical Punishments.
8vo, *net*, 2 50
—— Compendium Juris Canonici. 8vo, *net*, 2 00
—— The Marriage Process in the United States.
8vo, *net*, 2 50
SODALISTS' VADE MECUM. 32mo cloth, 0 50
SOUVENIR OF THE NOVITIATE. 32mo, *net*, 0 60
SPIRITUAL CRUMBS FOR HUNGRY LITTLE SOULS.
Richardson. 16mo, 0 50
STANG, Rev. William, D.D. Pastoral Theology.
New enlarged edition. 8vo, *net*, 1 50
STORIES FOR FIRST COMMUNICANTS. Keller.
32mo, 0 50
SUMMER AT WOODVILLE, A. Sadlier. 16mo, 0 50
SURE WAY TO A HAPPY MARRIAGE. Paper, 0.25;
per 100, 12.50; cloth, 0.35; per 100, 21 00
TANQUEREY, Rev. S. S. Synopsis Theologiæ
Fundamentalis. 8vo, *net*, 1 50
—— Synopsis Theologia Dogmatica Specialis. 2
vols. 8vo, *net*, 3 00
TALES AND LEGENDS OF THE MIDDLE AGES.
Capella. 16mo, 0 75
TAMING OF POLLY, THE. Dorsey. 12mo, 0 85
THREE GIRLS AND ESPECIALLY ONE. By M. A.
Taggart. 16mo, 0 50
THOUGHT FROM ST. ALPHONSUS, for Every Day.
32mo, 0 50
THOUGHT FROM BENEDICTINE SAINTS. 32mo, 0 50
THOUGHT FROM DOMINICAN SAINTS. 32mo, 0 50
THOUGHT FROM ST. FRANCIS ASSISI and his Saints.
32mo, 0 50
THOUGHT FROM ST. IGNATIUS. 32mo, 0 50
THOUGHT FROM ST. TERESA. 32mo, 0 50

THOUGHT FROM ST. VINCENT DE PAUL. 32mo, 0 50
TRUE POLITENESS. Addressed to Religious. By the Rev. Francis Demare. 16mo, *net*, 0 60
TRUE SPOUSE OF CHRIST. By St. Alphonsus Liguori. 2 vols., 12mo, *net*, 2.50; 1 vol., 12mo, *net*, 1 00
TRUTHS OF SALVATION. Pergmayr. 16mo, *net*, 0 75
TWELVE VIRTUES, THE, of a Good Teacher. For Mothers, Instructors, etc. Pottier. 32mo, *net*, 0 30
VISIT TO EUROPE AND THE HOLY LAND. Fairbanks. 12mo, illustrated, 1 50
VISITS TO THE MOST HOLY SACRAMENT, Liguori. 32mo, 0 50
VOCATION OF EDWARD CONWAY, THE. A Novel. By M. F. Egan. 12mo, 1 25
VOCATIONS EXPLAINED: Matrimony, Virginity, the Religious State, and the Priesthood. By a Vincentian Father. 16mo, flexible, 10 cents; per 100, 5 00
WARD, REV. THOMAS F. Fifty-two Instructions on the Principal Truths. 12mo, *net*, 0 75
—— Thirty-two Instructions for the Month of May. 12mo, *net*, 0 75
—— Month of May at Mary's Altar. 12mo, *net*, 0 75
—— Short Instructions for all the Sundays and Holydays. 12mo, *net*, 1 25
WAY OF THE CROSS. Illus. Paper, 5 cents; per 100, 3 00
WAY OF INTERIOR PEACE. De Lehen. 12mo, *net*, 1 25
WHAT CATHOLICS HAVE DONE FOR SCIENCE. Brennan. 12mo, 1 00
WOMAN OF FORTUNE, A. Reid. 12mo, cloth, 1 25
WOMEN OF CATHOLICITY. Sadlier. 12mo, 1 00
WORDS OF JESUS CHRIST DURING HIS PASSION. Schouppe, S.J. Flexible cloth, 0 25
WORDS OF WISDOM. A Concordance of the Sapiential Books. 12mo, *net*, 1 25
YOUNG GIRL'S BOOK OF PIETY. 16mo, 1 00
ZEAL IN THE WORK OF THE MINISTRY. Dubois. 8vo, *net*, 1 50

www.ingramcontent.com/pod-product-compliance
Lightning Source LLC
Chambersburg PA
CBHW031353230426
43670CB00006B/524